Table of Contents

Chapter 1: Introduction to SFML

1.1 What is SFML?

SFML, which stands for **Simple and Fast Multimedia Library**, is a popular and powerful open-source C++ library designed to facilitate game and multimedia development. It provides a wide range of features and tools that simplify the creation of interactive applications, including games, multimedia software, simulations, and more.

SFML is known for its simplicity and ease of use, making it an excellent choice for both beginners and experienced developers. It abstracts many complex aspects of multimedia programming, such as handling graphics, audio, and input, allowing developers to focus on game logic and creativity.

Key Features of SFML

SFML offers several key features that make it a valuable tool for game development:

- **Graphics:** SFML provides a simple and efficient graphics rendering system. You can easily create windows, draw shapes, display images, and manage 2D graphics with minimal effort.

- **Audio:** SFML supports various audio formats and allows you to play sound effects and music in your games. It also provides tools for controlling volume, pitch, and spatialization.

- **Input Handling:** SFML simplifies user input management by offering support for keyboards, mice, joysticks, and gamepads. You can easily detect and respond to user actions.

- **Window Management:** Creating and managing windows for your games or applications is straightforward with SFML. You can customize window properties and handle events like resizing and closing.

- **Cross-Platform:** SFML is designed to be cross-platform and works on Windows, macOS, Linux, and more. This means you can develop games that run on various operating systems without major code modifications.

- **Community and Support:** SFML has an active and supportive community, which means you can find tutorials, forums, and resources to help you along your development journey.

Why Choose SFML for Game Development?

SFML offers several compelling reasons to choose it for your game development projects:

1. **Ease of Use:** SFML's straightforward and well-documented API makes it accessible to developers of all skill levels. Beginners can quickly get started, while experienced developers appreciate its efficiency.

2. **Cross-Platform Compatibility:** SFML's cross-platform nature allows you to develop games that can be deployed on multiple operating systems, reaching a broader audience.

3. **Active Development:** SFML is actively maintained and updated, ensuring that it stays current with modern development practices and technology.

4. **Performance:** SFML is known for its performance and efficiency in rendering graphics and handling multimedia, making it suitable for both 2D and 3D game development.

5. **Community and Resources:** The SFML community provides a wealth of tutorials, forums, and third-party libraries to help you solve problems and enhance your projects.

In the following sections of this book, we will delve deeper into SFML, starting with setting up your development environment and installing SFML on various platforms. This will prepare you for creating your first SFML project and exploring the library's capabilities for game development.

1.2 Why Choose SFML for Game Development?

SFML offers several compelling advantages that make it an excellent choice for game development. In this section, we will explore some of the key reasons why you should consider using SFML for your game projects.

1. Cross-Platform Compatibility

One of the primary reasons to choose SFML is its cross-platform compatibility. SFML is designed to work seamlessly on multiple operating systems, including Windows, macOS, Linux, and more. This means that you can develop your game once and deploy it on various platforms without the need for extensive platform-specific code modifications. This not only saves time but also allows you to reach a broader audience.

2. Simplicity and Ease of Use

SFML is known for its simplicity and ease of use. It provides a clean and intuitive API that abstracts many of the complexities of multimedia programming. Whether you are a beginner or an experienced developer, you'll find SFML's API easy to understand and work with. This simplicity allows you to focus on game logic and creativity rather than struggling with intricate programming details.

3. Performance and Efficiency

Performance is a critical factor in game development, and SFML excels in this regard. It is designed to be efficient in rendering graphics, playing audio, and handling user input. SFML's lightweight design ensures that your games run smoothly, even on older hardware. This makes it suitable for both 2D and 3D game development projects.

4. Active Development and Community Support

SFML is actively developed and maintained by a dedicated team of developers. This ensures that the library stays up-to-date with modern development practices and technology. Additionally, SFML has a vibrant and supportive community. You can find a wealth of tutorials, forums, and third-party libraries created by fellow developers, making it easier to solve problems and enhance your game projects.

5. Extensive Features for Game Development

SFML provides a wide range of features tailored to game development. It includes built-in support for graphics rendering, audio playback, input handling (including keyboards, mice, joysticks, and gamepads), and window management. Additionally, SFML supports advanced features like networking, which is essential for multiplayer games, and shader programming for custom graphics effects.

6. Licensing and Open Source

SFML is an open-source library released under the zlib/png license, which allows you to use it in commercial and non-commercial projects without major licensing restrictions. This flexibility is advantageous for indie developers and small game studios looking to create games without high licensing costs.

In summary, SFML offers a compelling package of cross-platform compatibility, simplicity, performance, community support, extensive features, and open-source licensing. These factors make it a strong choice for game developers of all levels who are looking to create engaging and accessible games across different platforms. In the following chapters, we will dive deeper into using SFML to develop games, starting with setting up your development environment and getting your first SFML project up and running.

1.3 Setting Up Your Development Environment

Before you can start developing games with SFML, you need to set up your development environment. This involves preparing your computer and installing the necessary tools and libraries. In this section, we'll guide you through the steps to ensure your development environment is ready for SFML game development.

1.3.1 Choosing a C++ Compiler

SFML is a C++ library, so you'll need a C++ compiler to build and run your projects. The choice of compiler depends on your platform:

- **Windows:** You can use Visual C++ if you're on Windows. Alternatively, you can use MinGW, which provides a GCC-based compiler for Windows.

- **macOS:** Xcode, which includes the Clang compiler, is the preferred choice for macOS development. It comes bundled with essential tools for C++ development.

- **Linux:** On Linux, you can use GCC, which is a widely-used and well-supported C++ compiler.

Ensure that your chosen compiler is installed and configured correctly on your system. You can check this by opening a terminal or command prompt and running the compiler's version command (e.g., g++ --version for GCC).

1.3.2 Installing CMake

CMake is a cross-platform build system that simplifies the process of building and configuring your projects. SFML uses CMake for project generation and building. You can download and install CMake from the official website (https://cmake.org/download/). Be sure to add CMake to your system's PATH so that you can use it from the command line.

1.3.3 Downloading SFML

To get started with SFML, you'll need to download the library itself. Visit the official SFML website (https://www.sfml-dev.org/download.php) and select the appropriate version for your platform. You can choose between the stable and development versions. The stable version is recommended for most projects.

1.3.4 Building SFML (Optional)

SFML is distributed as pre-built binaries for most platforms, making it easy to get started. However, if you prefer to build SFML from source or if you need to customize the build, you can find the source code on the SFML GitHub repository (https://github.com/SFML/SFML). The repository includes build instructions for various platforms.

1.3.5 Setting Up a Project

With SFML downloaded and your development tools in place, you can start creating your first SFML project. Typically, you'll create a new CMake-based project and configure it to use SFML. Detailed instructions for setting up a project will be covered in later chapters, but the general steps involve creating a CMakeLists.txt file and linking your project with the SFML libraries.

1.3.6 IDEs and Text Editors

You can develop SFML projects using a variety of integrated development environments (IDEs) and text editors. Some popular options include Visual Studio (on Windows), Xcode (on macOS), Code::Blocks, CLion, and Visual Studio Code. These IDEs often provide code highlighting, debugging tools, and project management features that can streamline your development process.

1.3.7 Verifying Your Setup

Before you start writing code, it's a good practice to verify that your development environment is set up correctly. You can do this by creating a simple "Hello, SFML!" program to ensure that SFML libraries are properly linked and that you can build and run SFML applications.

In conclusion, setting up your development environment for SFML is a crucial initial step in your game development journey. It involves choosing a C++ compiler, installing CMake, downloading SFML, optionally building SFML from source, setting up your project, and selecting an IDE or text editor. Ensuring that your environment is configured correctly will save you time and frustration as you embark on creating exciting games using SFML.

1.4 Installing SFML on Windows

Installing SFML on Windows is a straightforward process, and it's the first step towards starting your game development journey with SFML. In this section, we'll guide you through the process of installing SFML on a Windows operating system.

1.4.1 Downloading SFML for Windows

To get started, visit the official SFML website (https://www.sfml-dev.org/download/sfml/2.5.1/) and download the SFML 2.5.1 Windows version. You can choose either the 32-bit or 64-bit version, depending on your system. If you're unsure, you can check your system type by right-clicking "This PC" or "My Computer" and selecting "Properties."

1.4.2 Extracting SFML

Once the download is complete, locate the downloaded SFML archive (usually a .zip file) and extract its contents to a directory of your choice. This directory will serve as your SFML installation directory.

1.4.3 Configuring Your Development Environment

To use SFML in your C++ projects, you need to configure your development environment to include the SFML headers and link against the SFML libraries. Follow these steps:

1. Inside the SFML installation directory, you'll find a folder named "include." This folder contains the SFML header files. Copy this "include" folder to a location where you keep your development headers.

1. In the SFML installation directory, you'll find a folder named "lib." Inside this folder, there are subfolders for each SFML module (e.g., "sfml-system," "sfml-graphics"). Each module folder contains the corresponding SFML library files.

2. Copy the library files from the module(s) you intend to use (e.g., "sfml-graphics.lib," "sfml-system.lib") to a location where you keep your development libraries.

If you're using an integrated development environment (IDE) like Visual Studio, you need to configure your project to include the SFML headers and link against the SFML libraries:

1. Open your project in Visual Studio.

2. Right-click on your project in the Solution Explorer and select "Properties."

3. In the project properties, navigate to "Configuration Properties" > "VC++ Directories."

4. In "Include Directories," add the path to the "include" folder where you copied the SFML headers.

5. In "Library Directories," add the path to the folder where you copied the SFML libraries.

6. Under "Configuration Properties" > "C/C++" > "General," you can add the same include directory path to "Additional Include Directories."

7. Under "Configuration Properties" > "Linker" > "General," add the path to the folder where you copied the SFML libraries to "Additional Library Directories."

8. Under "Configuration Properties" > "Linker" > "Input," add the names of the SFML libraries you intend to use (e.g., "sfml-graphics.lib," "sfml-system.lib") to "Additional Dependencies."

1.4.4 Verifying Your Setup

To ensure that your SFML setup on Windows is correct, you can create a simple "Hello, SFML!" program and build it. If everything is configured properly, you should be able to run the program without errors.

```
#include <SFML/Graphics.hpp>

int main()
```

```
{
    sf::RenderWindow window(sf::VideoMode(800, 600), "SFML Window");

    while (window.isOpen())
    {
        sf::Event event;
        while (window.pollEvent(event))
        {
            if (event.type == sf::Event::Closed)
                window.close();
        }

        window.clear();
        window.display();
    }

    return 0;
}
```

This program creates a window using SFML and keeps it open until you close it. If the window appears without any issues, congratulations! Your SFML installation on Windows is complete, and you're ready to start developing games with SFML.

In the following chapters, we'll explore how to use SFML to create games and multimedia applications on Windows and other platforms.

1.5 Installing SFML on Mac and Linux

Installing SFML on macOS and Linux is a crucial step in preparing your development environment for SFML-based game development. In this section, we'll guide you through the process of installing SFML on both macOS and Linux operating systems.

1.5.1 Installing SFML on macOS

To install SFML on macOS, you can use Homebrew, a popular package manager for macOS. Follow these steps to get SFML up and running:

1. Open the Terminal application on your macOS.

2. Install Homebrew if you haven't already by running the following command:

    ```
    /bin/bash -c "$(curl -fsSL https://raw.githubusercontent.com/Homebrew/install/master/install.sh)"
    ```

3. Once Homebrew is installed, you can install SFML by running the following command:

    ```
    brew install sfml
    ```

4. Homebrew will download and install the SFML library and its dependencies. This process may take a few moments.

5. After the installation is complete, you can verify the installation by checking the SFML version:

```
brew info sfml
```

This command should display information about the installed SFML package, including the version number.

1.5.2 Installing SFML on Linux

On Linux, the process of installing SFML varies depending on your distribution. Below, we provide instructions for installing SFML on two popular Linux distributions: Ubuntu and Fedora. If you're using a different distribution, you may need to adapt these instructions.

Installing SFML on Ubuntu

To install SFML on Ubuntu, open the Terminal and run the following commands:

1. Update the package list to ensure you have the latest information:

```
sudo apt update
```

2. Install SFML using the package manager:

```
sudo apt install libsfml-dev
```

3. After the installation is complete, you can verify the installation by checking the SFML version:

```
pkg-config --modversion sfml-all
```

Installing SFML on Fedora

To install SFML on Fedora, use the following commands in the Terminal:

1. Install SFML and its development packages:

```
sudo dnf install SFML SFML-devel
```

2. After the installation is complete, you can verify the installation by checking the SFML version:

```
pkg-config --modversion sfml-all
```

1.5.3 Verifying Your Setup

To ensure that your SFML setup on macOS or Linux is correct, you can create a simple "Hello, SFML!" program and build it. If everything is configured properly, you should be able to run the program without errors.

Here's a sample program:

```cpp
#include <SFML/Graphics.hpp>

int main()
{
    sf::RenderWindow window(sf::VideoMode(800, 600), "SFML Window");

    while (window.isOpen())
    {
        sf::Event event;
        while (window.pollEvent(event))
        {
            if (event.type == sf::Event::Closed)
                window.close();
        }

        window.clear();
        window.display();
    }

    return 0;
}
```

Compile the program using your preferred C++ compiler, and if the window appears without any issues, congratulations! Your SFML installation on macOS or Linux is complete, and you're ready to start developing games with SFML.

In the upcoming chapters, we'll explore how to utilize SFML to create games and multimedia applications on macOS, Linux, and other supported platforms.

Chapter 2: Getting Started with C++

2.1 Basics of C++ Programming

C++ is a powerful and versatile programming language widely used in game development, system programming, and various other fields. In this section, we'll cover the fundamental concepts and syntax of C++ to provide you with a strong foundation for working with SFML and game development.

2.1.1 What is C++?

C++ is an extension of the C programming language with added features that support object-oriented programming (OOP). It is known for its performance, efficiency, and low-level control, making it a popular choice for game development.

Here are some key characteristics of C++:

- **Compiled Language:** C++ is a compiled language, which means you write your code in a text editor and then compile it into an executable program using a compiler. This compilation process results in highly efficient machine code that can run directly on a computer.

- **Object-Oriented:** C++ supports OOP principles, allowing you to create classes and objects to structure your code. This approach promotes code reuse and modularity.

- **Strongly Typed:** C++ is a strongly typed language, which means you need to declare variable types explicitly. This helps catch type-related errors at compile time.

- **Low-Level and High-Level:** C++ provides low-level control over hardware resources, such as memory management, but also supports high-level abstractions like classes and templates.

2.1.2 Hello, World! in C++

Let's start with a classic "Hello, World!" program in C++. This program will introduce you to the basic structure of a C++ program.

```cpp
#include <iostream>

int main() {
    // This is a comment
    std::cout << "Hello, World!" << std::endl;
    return 0;
}
```

Here's a breakdown of the code:

- `#include <iostream>`: This line includes the input/output stream library, which provides functions for reading and writing data.

- `int main()`: Every C++ program begins with a `main` function. The `int` before `main` indicates that the function returns an integer value.

- `{}`: The curly braces `{}` enclose the body of the `main` function, where your program's statements go.

- `// This is a comment`: Comments in C++ start with `//` and are used for adding explanations or notes to your code. Comments are ignored by the compiler.

- `std::cout << "Hello, World!" << std::endl;`: This line uses `std::cout` (short for "console output") to display "Hello, World!" on the console. The `<<` operator is used to stream data to the console.

- `return 0;`: The `return` statement with a value of `0` indicates that the program has executed successfully.

2.1.3 Variables and Data Types

C++ supports various data types, including integers, floating-point numbers, characters, and more. You declare variables to store and manipulate data. Here are some common data types:

- `int`: Represents integers.
- `float` and `double`: Represent floating-point numbers (decimal numbers).
- `char`: Represents single characters.
- `bool`: Represents Boolean values (`true` or `false`).

Here's how you declare and initialize variables:

```
int age = 25;
float pi = 3.14159;
char grade = 'A';
bool isGameRunning = true;
```

You can perform arithmetic operations on numeric data types:

```
int x = 10;
int y = 5;
int sum = x + y;
int difference = x - y;
int product = x * y;
float quotient = static_cast<float>(x) / y; // Cast to float for accurate division
```

2.1.4 Control Structures

C++ provides control structures like if, else, for, while, and switch to control the flow of your program. Here's an example using if and else:

```cpp
int num = 42;
if (num > 50) {
    std::cout << "Num is greater than 50." << std::endl;
} else {
    std::cout << "Num is not greater than 50." << std::endl;
}
```

And here's a for loop:

```cpp
for (int i = 0; i < 5; i++) {
    std::cout << "Iteration " << i << std::endl;
}
```

2.1.5 Functions

Functions allow you to encapsulate and reuse blocks of code. You define a function with a name, parameters, and a body. Here's an example:

```cpp
int add(int a, int b) {
    return a + b;
}

int result = add(3, 4); // Calls the add function with arguments 3 and 4
```

In this section, we've covered the basics of C++ programming, including data types, variables, control structures, and functions. These concepts serve as the foundation for developing games with SFML, as you'll use C++ to create the game logic and interact with the SFML library. In the following chapters, we'll build upon this knowledge to create exciting games using SFML.

2.2 Object-Oriented Programming in C++

Object-oriented programming (OOP) is a programming paradigm that focuses on organizing code into reusable and maintainable structures called "objects." C++ is a powerful language that fully supports OOP principles. In this section, we'll explore the core concepts of OOP in C++ and how they are used in game development with SFML.

2.2.1 Classes and Objects

At the heart of OOP in C++ are classes and objects. A class is a blueprint for creating objects, and an object is an instance of a class. Classes define the properties (attributes) and behaviors (methods) that objects of that class will have.

Here's a simplified example of defining a class in C++:

```cpp
class Circle {
public:
    // Attributes
    float radius;

    // Constructor
    Circle(float r) {
        radius = r;
    }

    // Method to calculate area
    float calculateArea() {
        return 3.14159 * radius * radius;
    }
};
```

In this example, we define a `Circle` class with an attribute `radius`, a constructor to initialize the radius when an object is created, and a method `calculateArea()` to compute the area of the circle.

We can create objects of the `Circle` class like this:

```cpp
Circle smallCircle(2.0); // Create a Circle object with radius 2.0
Circle largeCircle(5.0); // Create a Circle object with radius 5.0

float smallArea = smallCircle.calculateArea(); // Calculate the area of the small circle
float largeArea = largeCircle.calculateArea(); // Calculate the area of the large circle
```

2.2.2 Encapsulation

Encapsulation is one of the core principles of OOP and involves bundling data (attributes) and methods (functions) that operate on that data into a single unit, the class. Encapsulation provides the following benefits:

- **Data Hiding:** Attributes of a class can be made private, meaning they can only be accessed and modified by methods within the class. This hides the implementation details and ensures data integrity.

- **Abstraction:** Abstraction allows you to define a simplified interface for a class, hiding complex implementation details. Users of the class interact with the public interface, not the internal workings.

Here's an example of encapsulation in C++:

```cpp
class Player {
private:
    int health; // Private attribute
```

```cpp
public:
    Player() {
        health = 100;
    }

    void takeDamage(int damage) {
        if (damage > 0) {
            health -= damage;
        }
    }

    int getHealth() {
        return health;
    }
};
```

In this example, the health attribute is private, so it can only be accessed or modified using the takeDamage() and getHealth() methods. This encapsulation prevents direct manipulation of the health attribute, ensuring that it stays within a valid range.

2.2.3 Inheritance

Inheritance is another fundamental concept of OOP that allows you to create a new class (derived class) based on an existing class (base class). The derived class inherits the attributes and methods of the base class and can add additional attributes or methods or override existing ones.

Here's an example of inheritance in C++:

```cpp
class Animal {
public:
    void eat() {
        std::cout << "Animal is eating." << std::endl;
    }
};

class Dog : public Animal {
public:
    void bark() {
        std::cout << "Dog is barking." << std::endl;
    }
};
```

In this example, the Dog class is derived from the Animal class. It inherits the eat() method from the Animal class and adds its own method, bark(). A Dog object can both eat and bark because it has access to both methods.

2.2.4 Polymorphism

Polymorphism is the ability of objects of different classes to respond to the same method call in a way that is appropriate for their specific class. In C++, polymorphism is often achieved through virtual functions and inheritance.

Here's an example of polymorphism in C++:

```cpp
class Shape {
public:
    virtual void draw() {
        std::cout << "Drawing a shape." << std::endl;
    }
};

class Circle : public Shape {
public:
    void draw() override {
        std::cout << "Drawing a circle." << std::endl;
    }
};

class Rectangle : public Shape {
public:
    void draw() override {
        std::cout << "Drawing a rectangle." << std::endl;
    }
};
```

In this example, we have a base class Shape with a virtual method draw(). Two derived classes, Circle and Rectangle, override the draw() method. When we call draw() on a Shape object, the appropriate version of draw() is executed based on the actual object's class.

```cpp
Shape* shape = new Circle();
shape->draw(); // Calls the draw() method of the Circle class

shape = new Rectangle();
shape->draw(); // Calls the draw() method of the Rectangle class
```

2.2.5 OOP in Game Development with SFML

Object-oriented programming is essential in game development with SFML. You can use classes and objects to represent game entities, such as characters, enemies, and items. Inheritance allows you to create specialized classes for different types of game objects, while polymorphism enables you to handle them uniformly in certain situations.

For example, you might create a base GameObject class with common attributes and behaviors shared by all game objects and then derive specific game object classes like Player, Enemy, and Item from it.

In this section, we've explored the core concepts of object-oriented programming in C++, including classes, objects, encapsulation, inheritance, and polymorphism. These concepts provide a structured and organized way to design and develop complex game systems in SFML, promoting code reusability and maintainability. In the following chapters, we'll apply these principles to create engaging games using SFML.

2.3 C++ Features for Game Development

C++ offers a wide range of features and capabilities that make it a popular choice for game development. In this section, we'll explore some of the key C++ features and how they benefit game development with SFML.

2.3.1 Performance and Efficiency

One of the most significant advantages of using C++ for game development is its performance and efficiency. C++ compiles to highly optimized machine code, making it well-suited for resource-intensive tasks like rendering complex graphics, physics simulations, and AI calculations. Games often demand real-time responsiveness, and C++ helps deliver that level of performance.

2.3.2 Memory Management

C++ provides direct control over memory management, allowing game developers to allocate and deallocate memory as needed. This control is crucial for avoiding memory leaks and optimizing memory usage in games, where efficient memory allocation is essential for performance.

Game developers can use features like pointers and manual memory management to fine-tune memory allocation for their specific requirements. Libraries like SFML handle many memory management tasks internally, but having control over memory allocation can be valuable for certain game elements.

2.3.3 Multiplatform Development

C++ is a cross-platform programming language, meaning you can write code that runs on various operating systems without significant modifications. This cross-platform compatibility is vital for game developers who want to target multiple platforms, such as Windows, macOS, Linux, and even mobile platforms like Android and iOS.

SFML, being a cross-platform multimedia library, complements C++ well by providing consistent APIs for different platforms. Game developers can write code once and deploy it on various systems, minimizing the effort required for porting games.

2.3.4 Object-Oriented Programming (OOP)

As discussed in the previous section, C++ fully supports OOP principles. Game development often involves managing numerous game objects with different properties and behaviors.

OOP allows developers to create modular and maintainable code by encapsulating game logic within classes and objects.

In the context of SFML game development, OOP facilitates the creation of game entities like characters, enemies, and items as objects. This organization makes it easier to manage complex game states and interactions.

2.3.5 Standard Template Library (STL)

C++ includes a powerful Standard Template Library (STL) that provides a collection of template classes and functions for common data structures and algorithms. The STL simplifies many programming tasks, such as managing collections, sorting data, and performing various operations on containers.

Game developers can leverage the STL to implement game-related data structures, like containers for storing game objects, collision detection, and AI decision-making. The use of well-tested and efficient STL components can save development time and improve code quality.

2.3.6 Libraries and Frameworks

C++ has a rich ecosystem of libraries and frameworks that cater to various aspects of game development. SFML itself is an example of such a library, providing essential features for 2D game development, including graphics rendering, window management, and input handling.

In addition to SFML, C++ game developers can explore other libraries and frameworks like SDL (Simple DirectMedia Layer), OpenGL for 3D graphics, and game engines such as Unreal Engine and Unity, which offer C++ scripting support. These tools extend C++'s capabilities for creating games with diverse requirements.

2.3.7 Community and Resources

C++ has a large and active community of developers and resources available online. This community provides tutorials, forums, and open-source projects related to game development, making it easier for newcomers to learn and get help when facing challenges.

SFML, specifically, has an active community with extensive documentation, forums, and a repository on GitHub. Game developers can benefit from the collective knowledge and support of the C++ and SFML communities.

In conclusion, C++ offers a robust set of features and advantages that make it an excellent choice for game development, particularly when combined with libraries like SFML. Its performance, memory management, cross-platform compatibility, and support for OOP and libraries like STL make C++ a powerful tool for creating engaging and efficient games. In the subsequent chapters, we'll put these C++ features to use as we delve into game development using SFML.

2.4 Essential C++ Concepts for SFML

Before diving into game development with SFML, it's crucial to understand some essential C++ concepts and techniques that you'll frequently encounter while working with the SFML library. These concepts will help you make the most out of SFML and write clean and efficient code for your games.

2.4.1 Header Files and Source Files

In C++, code is typically organized into header files (with a .h or .hpp extension) and source files (with a .cpp extension). Header files contain class declarations, function prototypes, and variable declarations, while source files contain the implementation of those declarations.

For example, you might have a header file Player.h with the declaration of a Player class and a source file Player.cpp with the actual implementation of the class methods.

Header file (Player.h):

```cpp
#pragma once

class Player {
public:
    Player(); // Constructor declaration
    void move(int x, int y); // Method declaration
private:
    int posX, posY; // Private member variables
};
```

Source file (Player.cpp):

```cpp
#include "Player.h"

Player::Player() {
    posX = 0;
    posY = 0;
}

void Player::move(int x, int y) {
    posX += x;
    posY += y;
}
```

2.4.2 Namespaces

C++ uses namespaces to prevent naming conflicts between different parts of your code. SFML uses the sf namespace for its classes and functions. You can access SFML classes by prefixing them with sf::.

For example, to use the `sf::RenderWindow` class from SFML, you'd write:

```
sf::RenderWindow window;
```

You can also use a `using` directive to avoid having to prefix every SFML class and function with `sf::`. However, be cautious when using this approach to prevent naming conflicts:

```
using namespace sf;

RenderWindow window;
```

2.4.3 Constructors and Destructors

Constructors are special member functions that get called when an object of a class is created. They initialize the object's attributes and allocate any necessary resources. SFML classes often have constructors that initialize their internal state.

Destructors, on the other hand, are called when an object is destroyed (usually when it goes out of scope). They are responsible for cleaning up any resources the object has acquired, such as memory or files.

2.4.4 Pointers and References

Pointers and references allow you to work with memory more efficiently and pass data between functions without making unnecessary copies. You'll often use pointers and references when working with SFML objects.

For example, to create a pointer to an `sf::RenderWindow`, you can do the following:

```
sf::RenderWindow* windowPtr = new sf::RenderWindow(sf::VideoMode(800, 600), "SFML Window");
```

To create a reference to an existing `sf::RenderWindow`, you can do:

```
sf::RenderWindow& windowRef = existingWindow;
```

2.4.5 Memory Management

SFML takes care of memory management for most of its objects. However, you should be aware of how and when objects are created and destroyed.

When you use `new` to create an SFML object, you're responsible for deleting it when you're done to prevent memory leaks. For example:

```
sf::RenderWindow* windowPtr = new sf::RenderWindow(sf::VideoMode(800, 600), "SFML Window");
// Use the windowPtr
delete windowPtr; // Don't forget to delete it
```

Alternatively, you can use smart pointers like `std::unique_ptr` or `std::shared_ptr` to manage memory automatically.

2.4.6 Error Handling

Error handling is essential in game development. SFML provides error codes and exceptions for reporting and handling errors.

For example, when loading a texture, you can check its status:

```cpp
sf::Texture texture;
if (!texture.loadFromFile("image.png")) {
    // Handle the error
}
```

Or you can use exceptions:

```cpp
try {
    sf::Texture texture;
    texture.loadFromFile("image.png");
} catch (const std::exception& e) {
    // Handle the exception
}
```

2.4.7 Resource Management

Games often involve managing a large number of resources like textures, fonts, and sounds. Proper resource management is crucial for performance and stability.

SFML provides resource management classes like sf::Texture, sf::Font, and sf::SoundBuffer that can load and manage resources efficiently. These classes handle resource loading and unloading automatically.

2.4.8 Event Handling

Event handling is a core part of game development with SFML. You'll frequently use event loops to process user input, manage game states, and respond to various events like keyboard presses, mouse clicks, and window events.

Here's a basic example of an SFML event loop:

```cpp
sf::RenderWindow window(sf::VideoMode(800, 600), "SFML Window");

while (window.isOpen()) {
    sf::Event event;
    while (window.pollEvent(event)) {
        if (event.type == sf::Event::Closed) {
            window.close();
        }
    }
}
```

This loop continuously checks for events and responds to the "Closed" event by closing the window.

In summary, understanding these essential C++ concepts and techniques is vital for effective game development with SFML. They provide a solid foundation for working with the SFML library and creating robust and efficient games. In the upcoming chapters, we'll apply these concepts to build interactive and engaging games using SFML.

2.5 Creating Your First C++ Program

Now that we've covered some essential C++ concepts, it's time to create your first C++ program. We'll walk through the process of setting up a development environment, writing a simple C++ program, and compiling and running it.

2.5.1 Setting Up Your Development Environment

Before you can write and run C++ code, you need a development environment. Here are the basic steps to set up your development environment:

1. **Install a C++ Compiler:** You'll need a C++ compiler to translate your code into machine-readable instructions. Popular C++ compilers include GCC (GNU Compiler Collection) for Linux, Clang for macOS, and MinGW for Windows. You can also use an Integrated Development Environment (IDE) like Visual Studio or Code::Blocks that includes a C++ compiler.

2. **Choose a Text Editor or IDE:** You can write C++ code in a simple text editor like Notepad (Windows) or use a specialized code editor or IDE. IDEs like Visual Studio and Code::Blocks provide features like code highlighting, auto-completion, and debugging tools that can make your development process more efficient.

3. **Create a Workspace:** Organize your project files in a directory or folder. This will help keep your code organized and make it easier to manage your project.

2.5.2 Writing Your First C++ Program

Let's create a simple "Hello, World!" program in C++. This program will display a message on the console when executed.

```cpp
#include <iostream>

int main() {
    // This is a comment
    std::cout << "Hello, World!" << std::endl;
    return 0;
}
```

Here's what this code does:

- `#include <iostream>`: This line includes the input/output stream library, which provides functions for reading and writing data.

- `int main()`: Every C++ program begins with a `main` function. The `int` before `main` indicates that the function returns an integer value.

- `{}`: The curly braces `{}` enclose the body of the `main` function, where your program's statements go.

- `// This is a comment`: Comments in C++ start with `//` and are used for adding explanations or notes to your code. Comments are ignored by the compiler.

- `std::cout << "Hello, World!" << std::endl;`: This line uses `std::cout` (short for "console output") to display "Hello, World!" on the console. The `<<` operator is used to stream data to the console.

- `return 0;`: The `return` statement with a value of `0` indicates that the program has executed successfully.

2.5.3 Compiling and Running Your Program

Once you've written your C++ program, you need to compile it into an executable file. The compilation process translates your human-readable code into machine code that the computer can understand.

Here are the steps to compile and run your program using a command-line interface:

1. **Save Your Code:** Save your C++ program with a `.cpp` file extension, such as `hello.cpp`.

2. **Open a Terminal or Command Prompt:** Open a terminal window or command prompt on your computer.

3. **Navigate to Your Project Directory:** Use the `cd` command to navigate to the directory where you saved your C++ program. For example, if you saved it on your desktop, you can navigate there by running `cd Desktop`.

4. **Compile Your Program:** Use the appropriate command for your compiler. For GCC, you can use the following command:

```
g++ hello.cpp -o hello
```

This command tells the compiler (`g++`) to compile `hello.cpp` and create an output file named `hello`.

5. **Run Your Program:** After successful compilation, you can run your program by entering:

```
./hello
```

You should see the "Hello, World!" message displayed on the console.

2.5.4 Using an Integrated Development Environment (IDE)

If you prefer to use an IDE, the process of creating and running your first C++ program is typically more straightforward. Here's a general overview:

1. **Install an IDE:** Download and install a C++ IDE like Visual Studio, Code::Blocks, or another preferred option.

2. **Create a New Project:** Open your IDE and create a new C++ project. Most IDEs provide project templates for console applications.

3. **Write Your Code:** Use the IDE's code editor to write your C++ program.

4. **Compile and Run:** Use the IDE's build and run commands to compile and execute your program. The IDE typically handles the compilation and execution process for you.

2.5.5 Troubleshooting

If you encounter errors during compilation or execution, double-check your code for syntax errors and ensure that your development environment is set up correctly. Common issues include typos, missing semicolons, or incorrect compiler configurations.

Congratulations! You've successfully created and run your first C++ program. This is a significant milestone on your journey to game development with SFML. In the upcoming chapters, you'll build on this foundation to create interactive games using C++ and the SFML library.

Chapter 3: Your First SFML Project

3.1 Creating a Blank SFML Project

In this chapter, we will begin our journey into game development with SFML by creating your first SFML project. Before diving into the complexities of game development, it's essential to set up a basic project structure and get familiar with the essential components of an SFML application.

3.1.1 Installing SFML

Before you can create an SFML project, you need to ensure that SFML is correctly installed on your development environment. Here are the steps to install SFML:

1. **Download SFML:** Visit the SFML website and download the SFML library for your specific platform. Make sure to download the correct version (32-bit or 64-bit) that matches your development environment.

2. **Extract SFML:** Once you've downloaded SFML, extract the contents of the downloaded archive to a location on your computer.

3. **Link SFML:** To use SFML in your C++ project, you need to link the SFML libraries to your project. The specific steps for linking SFML depend on your development environment. Consult the SFML documentation or your IDE's documentation for detailed instructions on how to link SFML.

3.1.2 Creating a Blank SFML Project

Now that you have SFML installed, let's create a blank SFML project. In this section, we'll create a simple SFML application that opens a blank window. This is the starting point for most SFML projects.

Here's a basic structure for your SFML project:

```
SFML_Project/
│
├── main.cpp
├── CMakeLists.txt
├── assets/
│   └── (put your game assets here)
│
└── bin/
    └── (executable will be generated here)
```

- `main.cpp`: This is the main C++ source file for your SFML application.

- `CMakeLists.txt`: If you're using CMake for project configuration, this file specifies how your project should be built.

- **assets/**: This directory is where you should store your game assets, such as images, sounds, and fonts.

- **bin/**: This is where the executable for your SFML project will be generated.

Here's a minimal main.cpp file to create a blank SFML window:

```cpp
#include <SFML/Graphics.hpp>

int main() {
    sf::RenderWindow window(sf::VideoMode(800, 600), "SFML Window");

    while (window.isOpen()) {
        sf::Event event;
        while (window.pollEvent(event)) {
            if (event.type == sf::Event::Closed) {
                window.close();
            }
        }

        window.clear();
        // Add your game rendering code here
        window.display();
    }

    return 0;
}
```

In this code:

- We include the necessary SFML header <SFML/Graphics.hpp>.

- In the main() function, we create an sf::RenderWindow object, which represents our application window.

- Inside the main loop, we check for window closure events. If the user clicks the close button, we close the window.

- We clear the window using window.clear() and display any game rendering code in this section.

- Finally, we call window.display() to render the frame.

3.1.3 Running Your Blank SFML Project

To run your blank SFML project, follow these steps:

1. Open your terminal or command prompt and navigate to the directory where your project is located.

2. Build your project using your chosen build system (e.g., CMake or your IDE's build tools).

3. After a successful build, run the executable generated in the bin/ directory.

You should see a blank SFML window open. You can close the window by clicking the close button.

Congratulations! You've created and run your first SFML project. This basic setup provides a foundation for building more complex games using SFML. In the following sections of this chapter, we'll explore various aspects of SFML, such as graphics rendering, user input handling, and game development techniques to create interactive and engaging games.

3.2 Understanding the SFML Window

In the previous section, we created a blank SFML project and briefly introduced the sf::RenderWindow class for creating a window. In this section, we will delve deeper into understanding the SFML window and its essential properties.

3.2.1 Window Creation

As mentioned earlier, the sf::RenderWindow class is used to create and manage the application window. It takes two main arguments in its constructor:

- sf::VideoMode: This specifies the dimensions (width and height) of the window and the color depth (bits per pixel). For example, sf::VideoMode(800, 600, 32) creates a window with a width of 800 pixels, a height of 600 pixels, and a color depth of 32 bits per pixel.

- std::string: This argument is the title of the window, which appears in the window's title bar.

Here's an example of creating an SFML window with a specific size and title:

```
sf::RenderWindow window(sf::VideoMode(800, 600), "SFML Window");
```

3.2.2 Window Events

The SFML window allows you to respond to various events, such as mouse clicks, keyboard presses, and window closure. To handle these events, you typically use a game loop that continuously polls for events.

In the previous code example, we used a nested while loop to handle events:

```
while (window.isOpen()) {
    sf::Event event;
    while (window.pollEvent(event)) {
        if (event.type == sf::Event::Closed) {
            window.close();
```

```
        }
    }

    // Game Logic and rendering go here

    window.display();
}
```

- The outer loop (while (window.isOpen())) ensures that the window remains open as long as the application is running.

- The inner loop (while (window.pollEvent(event))) checks for pending events. When an event occurs, it's stored in the sf::Event object event.

- Inside the inner loop, we check if the event type is sf::Event::Closed, which corresponds to the user clicking the close button of the window. If this event is detected, we close the window using window.close().

This event handling structure allows you to respond to various user interactions and control the flow of your application.

3.2.3 Window Properties

SFML provides several methods to customize the window's appearance and behavior. Here are some common window properties you can set:

- **Window Position**: You can set the position of the window using the setPosition() method. For example, window.setPosition(sf::Vector2i(100, 100)) sets the window's position to (100, 100) pixels from the top-left corner of the screen.

- **Window Size**: The setSize() method allows you to change the size of the window. For example, window.setSize(sf::Vector2u(1024, 768)) sets the window's size to 1024x768 pixels.

- **Window Style**: SFML supports various window styles, such as borderless, resizable, and fullscreen. You can set the window style using the setStyle() method. For example, window.setStyle(sf::Style::Fullscreen) makes the window fullscreen.

- **Frame Rate Limit**: You can limit the frame rate of your application using the setFramerateLimit() method. For example, window.setFramerateLimit(60) limits the frame rate to 60 frames per second (FPS).

3.2.4 Clearing and Displaying the Window

To render graphics in the SFML window, you need to follow a common rendering pattern within your game loop:

1. **Clear the Window**: Before rendering a new frame, use window.clear() to clear the previous frame's contents. This is typically done at the beginning of your game loop.

2. **Render Your Game**: Between clearing the window and displaying the window, you add your game's rendering code. This can involve drawing sprites, shapes, text, and other graphical elements.

3. **Display the Window**: Finally, use `window.display()` to present the rendered frame to the user.

Here's a simplified example:

```
while (window.isOpen()) {
    // Clear the window
    window.clear();

    // Game Logic and rendering go here
    // (e.g., draw shapes, sprites, and text)

    // Display the window
    window.display();
}
```

This pattern ensures that you always have a clean canvas to render your game's visuals.

3.2.5 Closing the Window

To close the SFML window, you can use the `window.close()` method as demonstrated in the event handling section. Alternatively, you can also use other methods like pressing the window's close button or pressing a specific key combination based on your event handling logic.

In summary, understanding the SFML window is crucial for creating graphical applications and games. You've learned how to create a window, handle events, customize window properties, and follow a rendering pattern. With this knowledge, you're well-equipped to begin developing interactive and visually appealing games using SFML. In the upcoming sections of this chapter, we'll explore more advanced graphics and game development concepts with SFML.

3.3 Displaying Graphics with SFML

In the previous sections, we've set up a blank SFML project and explored the basics of window creation and event handling. Now, let's dive into the exciting world of graphics rendering with SFML. SFML provides a versatile set of tools and features for creating 2D graphics, making it a popular choice for 2D game development.

3.3.1 The SFML Graphics Module

SFML's graphics functionality is primarily provided by the `sf::Graphics` module. This module includes classes and functions for drawing shapes, rendering text, working with sprites and textures, and managing the overall graphical aspects of your application.

Here's a brief overview of some of the key components of the SFML graphics module:

- **Shapes**: SFML provides various shape classes, such as `sf::RectangleShape`, `sf::CircleShape`, and `sf::ConvexShape`, which allow you to draw simple geometric shapes.

- **Sprites and Textures**: You can use the `sf::Sprite` class to display images or textures in your application. Textures can be loaded from image files and assigned to sprites for rendering.

- **Text Rendering**: The `sf::Text` class allows you to display text in different fonts and styles.

- **Transformations**: SFML supports various transformations like rotation, scaling, and translation, which can be applied to shapes, sprites, or the entire window.

3.3.2 Drawing Shapes

Drawing basic shapes in SFML is straightforward. You create an instance of the shape you want to draw, set its properties, and then draw it onto the SFML window. Here's a basic example of drawing a red rectangle:

```cpp
#include <SFML/Graphics.hpp>

int main() {
    sf::RenderWindow window(sf::VideoMode(800, 600), "SFML Shapes");

    while (window.isOpen()) {
        sf::Event event;
        while (window.pollEvent(event)) {
            if (event.type == sf::Event::Closed) {
                window.close();
            }
        }

        // Clear the window
        window.clear();

        // Create and configure a red rectangle
        sf::RectangleShape redRectangle;
        redRectangle.setSize(sf::Vector2f(100.0f, 100.0f));
        redRectangle.setFillColor(sf::Color::Red);

        // Draw the red rectangle
        window.draw(redRectangle);

        // Display the window
        window.display();
    }
```

```
    return 0;
}
```

In this example:

- We create an `sf::RenderWindow` as before.
- Inside the game loop, we create an `sf::RectangleShape` object named `redRectangle`.
- We set the size of the rectangle using `setSize()`, and we set its fill color to red using `setFillColor()`.
- We then draw the `redRectangle` onto the window using `window.draw(redRectangle)`.

This simple example demonstrates how to draw a basic shape, and you can extend this to draw other shapes like circles, polygons, or custom shapes as needed.

3.3.3 Drawing Sprites

In addition to basic shapes, SFML allows you to draw sprites, which are textured images. To draw a sprite, you'll typically load an image (texture) and create an `sf::Sprite` object to display it. Here's a basic example of drawing a sprite:

```cpp
#include <SFML/Graphics.hpp>

int main() {
    sf::RenderWindow window(sf::VideoMode(800, 600), "SFML Sprite");

    // Load a texture from an image file
    sf::Texture texture;
    if (!texture.loadFromFile("sprite.png")) {
        return 1; // Exit if the texture fails to load
    }

    // Create a sprite and set its texture
    sf::Sprite sprite;
    sprite.setTexture(texture);

    while (window.isOpen()) {
        sf::Event event;
        while (window.pollEvent(event)) {
            if (event.type == sf::Event::Closed) {
                window.close();
            }
        }

        // Clear the window
        window.clear();
```

```
        // Draw the sprite
        window.draw(sprite);

        // Display the window
        window.display();
    }

    return 0;
}
```

In this code:

- We load a texture from an image file using `texture.loadFromFile()`. Make sure to replace "sprite.png" with the path to your image file.

- We create an `sf::Sprite` named `sprite` and set its texture using `sprite.setTexture()`.

- Inside the game loop, we draw the `sprite` onto the window, just like we did with shapes.

3.3.4 Transformations

SFML provides methods to apply transformations to shapes and sprites. These transformations include rotation, scaling, and translation (positioning). For instance, you can rotate a sprite using `sprite.setRotation()`, scale it using `sprite.setScale()`, or move it to a new position with `sprite.setPosition()`.

Here's an example of rotating a sprite:

```
// Rotate the sprite by 45 degrees
sprite.setRotation(45);
```

And here's an example of scaling a sprite:

```
// Scale the sprite to double its size
sprite.setScale(2.0f, 2.0f);
```

Transformations can be combined to create complex animations or effects in your games.

3.3.5 Text Rendering

SFML makes it easy to render text on the screen. You can create an `sf::Text` object, set its font, size, and color, and then draw it onto the window.

Here's a simple example:

```
#include <SFML/Graphics.hpp>

int main() {
    sf::RenderWindow window(sf::VideoMode(800, 600), "SFML Text");
```

```
    // Create a font
    sf::Font font;
    if (!font.loadFromFile("arial.ttf")) {
        return 1; // Exit if the font fails to load
    }

    // Create a text object and set its properties
    sf::Text text("Hello, SFML!", font, 24);
    text.setFillColor(sf::Color::Green);

    while (window.isOpen()) {
        sf::Event event;
        while (window.pollEvent(event)) {
            if (event.type == sf::Event::Closed) {
                window.close();
            }
        }

        // Clear the window
        window.clear();

        // Draw the text
        window.draw(text);

        // Display the window
        window.display();
    }

    return 0;
}
```

In this example:

- We load a font from a file using `font.loadFromFile()`. You'll need to replace `"arial.ttf"` with the path to a TrueType font file on your system.

- We create an `sf::Text` object named `text` and set its string content, font, size, and fill color.

- Inside the game loop, we draw the `text` onto the window.

This demonstrates how to render text in your SFML applications, which can be used for game menus, score displays, and more.

3.3.6 Conclusion

SFML's graphics module provides a powerful and versatile set of tools for creating 2D graphics and visual elements in your games and applications. In this section, we've explored drawing basic shapes, displaying textured sprites, applying transformations, and rendering text. These are fundamental concepts that you'll

3.4 Handling User Input

User input is a fundamental aspect of game development, as it allows players to interact with the game world. SFML provides robust mechanisms for handling various types of user input, including keyboard, mouse, joystick, and touchscreen events. In this section, we'll explore how to handle user input in your SFML applications.

3.4.1 Keyboard Input Handling

Handling keyboard input in SFML is straightforward. You can check for key presses and releases in your game loop using the `sf::Keyboard` class. Here's a basic example of checking if the "W" key is pressed to move an object upward:

```cpp
#include <SFML/Graphics.hpp>

int main() {
    sf::RenderWindow window(sf::VideoMode(800, 600), "SFML Keyboard Input");

    sf::RectangleShape player(sf::Vector2f(50, 50));
    player.setFillColor(sf::Color::Blue);

    while (window.isOpen()) {
        sf::Event event;
        while (window.pollEvent(event)) {
            if (event.type == sf::Event::Closed) {
                window.close();
            }
        }

        // Handle keyboard input
        if (sf::Keyboard::isKeyPressed(sf::Keyboard::W)) {
            // Move the player upward
            player.move(0, -5);
        }

        // Clear the window
        window.clear();

        // Draw the player
        window.draw(player);

        // Display the window
        window.display();
    }
}
```

```
    return 0;
}
```

In this code:

- We create an `sf::RenderWindow` and a blue rectangle (`player`) that represents the player character.

- Inside the game loop, we check for key presses using `sf::Keyboard::isKeyPressed()`. If the "W" key is pressed, we move the `player` upward by changing its position using `player.move()`.

- You can adapt this approach to handle other keys and perform various actions in response to user input.

3.4.2 Mouse Input Handling

SFML also provides support for handling mouse input events. You can detect mouse button presses, releases, and movements. Here's an example of tracking the mouse position and drawing a shape where the mouse is clicked:

```cpp
#include <SFML/Graphics.hpp>

int main() {
    sf::RenderWindow window(sf::VideoMode(800, 600), "SFML Mouse Input");

    sf::CircleShape circle(20);
    circle.setFillColor(sf::Color::Red);

    while (window.isOpen()) {
        sf::Event event;
        while (window.pollEvent(event)) {
            if (event.type == sf::Event::Closed) {
                window.close();
            }

            // Handle mouse input
            if (event.type == sf::Event::MouseButtonPressed) {
                if (event.mouseButton.button == sf::Mouse::Left) {
                    // Get the mouse position and set the circle's position
                    sf::Vector2i mousePosition = sf::Mouse::getPosition(window);
                    circle.setPosition(static_cast<sf::Vector2f>(mousePosition));
                }
            }
        }

        // Clear the window
```

```
        window.clear();

        // Draw the circle
        window.draw(circle);

        // Display the window
        window.display();
    }

    return 0;
}
```

In this code:

- We create an `sf::RenderWindow` and a red circle (`circle`) that will follow the mouse when the left mouse button is clicked.

- Inside the game loop, we handle mouse input by checking if the left mouse button is pressed (`sf::Event::MouseButtonPressed`) and updating the position of the `circle` to the current mouse position.

- This allows you to create interactive elements in your games that respond to mouse clicks.

3.4.3 Joystick and Gamepad Support

SFML provides support for handling input from joysticks and gamepads. You can detect connected joysticks, read button and axis states, and respond to controller input. Here's a basic example of checking the state of the first connected joystick:

```cpp
#include <SFML/Graphics.hpp>

int main() {
    sf::RenderWindow window(sf::VideoMode(800, 600), "SFML Joystick Input");

    while (window.isOpen()) {
        sf::Event event;
        while (window.pollEvent(event)) {
            if (event.type == sf::Event::Closed) {
                window.close();
            }
        }

        // Handle joystick input
        if (sf::Joystick::isConnected(0)) {
            // Check if button 0 (A button on an Xbox controller) is pressed
            if (sf::Joystick::isButtonPressed(0, 0)) {
                // Perform an action
            }
```

```
        // Read the position of the left analog stick
        float xAxis = sf::Joystick::getAxisPosition(0, sf::Joystick::X);
        float yAxis = sf::Joystick::getAxisPosition(0, sf::Joystick::Y);

        // Use the axis values for game control
    }

    // Clear the window
    window.clear();

    // Display the window
    window.display();
    }

    return 0;
}
```

In this code:

- We create an `sf::RenderWindow` as usual.

- Inside the game loop, we check if a joystick is connected using
  `sf::Joystick::isConnected()`. Then, we check if a specific button (in this case,
  button 0) is pressed using `sf::Joystick::isButtonPressed()`.

- We also read the position of the left analog stick using
  `sf::Joystick::getAxisPosition()`.

- This allows you to integrate joystick and gamepad support into your games for a
  more immersive experience.

3.4.4 Implementing Touchscreen Controls

For mobile and touchscreen devices, SFML provides support for handling touch events. You
can detect touch events, get the position of touch points, and respond to touch-based
interactions.

Here's a simplified example of handling touch events:

```
#include <SFML/Graphics.hpp>

int main() {
    sf::RenderWindow window(sf::VideoMode(800, 600), "SFML Touchscreen Input"
);

    while (window.isOpen()) {
        sf::Event event;
```

##

3.5 Running Your First SFML Game

Now that we've covered the basics of setting up an SFML project, creating a window, rendering graphics, and handling user input, it's time to put it all together and create a simple SFML game. In this section, we'll walk through the process of building a classic game of Pong, which is an excellent starting point for learning game development with SFML.

3.5.1 The Pong Game

Pong is a classic 2D arcade game that simulates table tennis. In Pong, two players control paddles on opposite sides of the screen. A ball bounces back and forth between the paddles, and the players must use their paddles to hit the ball and prevent it from passing them. The objective is to score points by making the ball pass the opponent's paddle.

3.5.2 Game Components

Before diving into the code, let's outline the essential components of our Pong game:

- **Paddles**: There are two paddles, one for each player. The paddles can move vertically to hit the ball.

- **Ball**: The ball moves horizontally and vertically, bouncing off the paddles and the top and bottom edges of the screen.

- **Score**: The game keeps track of each player's score.

- **Game Over**: The game ends when one player reaches a certain score limit (e.g., 5 points).

3.5.3 Game Loop

The core of any game is its game loop, which repeatedly updates the game's state and renders it on the screen. In our Pong game, the game loop will perform the following steps:

1. Handle user input to move the paddles.
2. Update the ball's position based on its velocity.
3. Check for collisions between the ball and paddles, as well as with the screen edges.
4. Update the score if the ball goes past a paddle.
5. Draw the paddles, ball, and score on the screen.
6. Check if the game is over, and if so, display the winner.

Here's a simplified outline of what the game loop might look like:

```cpp
```

```
while (window.isOpen()) {
    // Handle user input
    // Update ball position
    // Check for collisions
    // Update score
    // Clear the window
    // Draw paddles, ball, and score
    // Check for game over
    // Display the window
}
```

In the following sections, we'll break down each of these steps and provide code examples for implementing them in SFML. By the end of this section, you'll have a working Pong game that you can play and further enhance with additional features and improvements. Let's get started!

Chapter 4: Setting Up a Cross-Platform Development Environment

4.1 Developing on Windows

When developing games or applications with SFML, you have the flexibility to work on different platforms, including Windows. Setting up your development environment on Windows is a crucial first step in your SFML journey. In this section, we'll guide you through the process of setting up SFML on a Windows system.

4.1.1 Installing a C++ Compiler

Before you can start using SFML, you need a C++ compiler. On Windows, one of the most popular choices is Visual Studio. Here's how you can set up Visual Studio for C++ development:

1. **Install Visual Studio**: Download and install Visual Studio from the official website (https://visualstudio.microsoft.com/).

2. **Select C++ Workload**: During installation, make sure to select the "Desktop development with C++" workload. This includes the necessary tools and libraries for C++ development.

3. **Install Desktop Development with C++**: In the Visual Studio Installer, you can further customize your installation by selecting specific components. Ensure that "Desktop development with C++" is selected.

4. **Optional: Install Visual C++ Redistributable**: Depending on your project, you might need to install the Visual C++ Redistributable package. You can find this package on the Microsoft website.

4.1.2 Setting Up SFML

Once you have a C++ development environment, it's time to set up SFML. Here are the steps to do so:

1. **Download SFML**: Go to the official SFML website (https://www.sfml-dev.org/) and navigate to the "Download" section. Download the SFML SDK for Windows.

2. **Extract SFML**: Extract the downloaded SFML archive to a directory of your choice. This directory will be referred to as your "SFML root directory."

3. **Link SFML in Your Project**: In your Visual Studio project, you need to specify the include directories, library directories, and link SFML libraries. Here's how to do it:
   - Open your project in Visual Studio.
   - Right-click on your project in the Solution Explorer and select "Properties."
   - Under "Configuration Properties," go to "VC++ Directories."

- Add the path to the "include" directory in your SFML root directory to "Include Directories."
- Under "Configuration Properties," go to "Linker" > "General."
- Add the path to the "lib" directory in your SFML root directory to "Additional Library Directories."
- Under "Configuration Properties," go to "Linker" > "Input."
- Add the names of the SFML libraries you're using to "Additional Dependencies." For example, if you're using SFML Graphics, add "sfml-graphics.lib."

4. **Copy DLLs**: To run your SFML application, you need to copy the required DLLs from the SFML root directory to your project's output directory. These DLLs can be found in the "bin" directory of your SFML installation.

4.1.3 Creating Your First SFML Project

With SFML and your development environment set up, you can create your first SFML project in Visual Studio. Here's a simple example of a Hello World program using SFML:

```cpp
#include <SFML/Graphics.hpp>

int main() {
    sf::RenderWindow window(sf::VideoMode(800, 600), "SFML Hello World");

    while (window.isOpen()) {
        sf::Event event;
        while (window.pollEvent(event)) {
            if (event.type == sf::Event::Closed) {
                window.close();
            }
        }

        window.clear();
        // Draw your graphics here
        window.display();
    }

    return 0;
}
```

This minimal SFML program creates a window, handles the close event, clears the window, and displays it. You can now start adding graphics, handling input, and building your games or applications on Windows using SFML.

In the next sections, we'll explore setting up SFML on Mac and Linux systems, as well as configuring code editors and IDEs for cross-platform development with SFML.

4.2 Developing on Mac

SFML is a versatile library that can be used for game development on Mac. Setting up your development environment on a Mac is essential to start creating games or applications with SFML. In this section, we'll guide you through the process of setting up SFML on a macOS system.

4.2.1 Installing a C++ Compiler

To begin developing with SFML on macOS, you'll need a C++ compiler. Xcode, the official development environment for macOS, includes the necessary tools for C++ development. Here's how to set it up:

1. **Install Xcode**: If you don't have Xcode installed, you can download it from the Mac App Store or the Apple Developer website (https://developer.apple.com/xcode/).

2. **Install Command Line Tools**: After installing Xcode, open Terminal and run the following command to install the Xcode Command Line Tools, which include the C++ compiler:

   xcode-select --install

   Follow the on-screen instructions to complete the installation.

4.2.2 Setting Up SFML

Once you have Xcode and the Command Line Tools installed, you can proceed to set up SFML. Here are the steps to do so:

1. **Download SFML**: Go to the official SFML website (https://www.sfml-dev.org/) and navigate to the "Download" section. Download the SFML SDK for macOS.

2. **Extract SFML**: Extract the downloaded SFML archive to a directory of your choice. This directory will be referred to as your "SFML root directory."

3. **Link SFML in Your Xcode Project**: To use SFML in your Xcode project, you need to link the SFML libraries and specify the include directories. Here's how to do it:

   - Open your Xcode project.

   - In the Project Navigator, right-click on your project and select "New Group." Name it "SFML."

   - Drag and drop the "include" directory from your SFML root directory into the "SFML" group in Xcode. This adds the SFML headers to your project.

   - In Xcode, navigate to your project's settings.

- Under "Build Settings," go to "Header Search Paths." Add the path to the "include" directory in your SFML root directory. Make sure to set it to "recursive."

- Under "Build Settings," go to "Library Search Paths." Add the path to the "lib" directory in your SFML root directory.

- Under "Build Phases," expand "Link Binary with Libraries" and click the "+" button to add the SFML libraries you're using. For example, if you're using SFML Graphics, add "libsfml-graphics.dylib."

4.2.3 Creating Your First SFML Project in Xcode

Now that you have SFML set up in your Xcode project, you can create your first SFML program. Here's a simple example of a Hello World program using SFML:

```cpp
#include <SFML/Graphics.hpp>

int main() {
    sf::RenderWindow window(sf::VideoMode(800, 600), "SFML Hello World");

    while (window.isOpen()) {
        sf::Event event;
        while (window.pollEvent(event)) {
            if (event.type == sf::Event::Closed) {
                window.close();
            }
        }

        window.clear();
        // Draw your graphics here
        window.display();
    }

    return 0;
}
```

This basic SFML program creates a window, handles the close event, clears the window, and displays it. You can start adding your graphics, handling input, and building your games or applications on macOS using SFML.

In the next section, we'll explore setting up SFML on Linux systems, as well as configuring code editors and IDEs for cross-platform development with SFML.

4.3 Developing on Linux

Linux is a popular platform for game development with SFML due to its flexibility and open-source nature. Setting up your development environment on a Linux system is crucial to start creating games or applications with SFML. In this section, we'll guide you through the process of setting up SFML on a Linux distribution.

4.3.1 Installing a C++ Compiler

Linux distributions usually come with a C++ compiler pre-installed. The most commonly used C++ compiler on Linux is GCC (GNU Compiler Collection). To check if GCC is installed, open a terminal and run the following command:

```
g++ --version
```

If GCC is not installed, you can install it using your distribution's package manager. For example, on Ubuntu or Debian-based systems, you can use:

```
sudo apt-get update
sudo apt-get install g++
```

For Red Hat-based systems like Fedora, you can use:

```
sudo dnf install gcc-c++
```

4.3.2 Setting Up SFML

Setting up SFML on Linux is straightforward, and you can do it using your distribution's package manager or by building SFML from source. Here are two common methods:

Method 1: Using the Package Manager

Many Linux distributions provide pre-built SFML packages that you can install using your package manager. These packages often include development libraries and headers. To install SFML via the package manager, open a terminal and use the following commands based on your distribution:

For Ubuntu/Debian:

```
sudo apt-get update
sudo apt-get install libsfml-dev
```

For Fedora:

```
sudo dnf install SFML-devel
```

Method 2: Building SFML from Source

If you prefer to build SFML from source, follow these steps:

1. **Download SFML**: Visit the official SFML website (https://www.sfml-dev.org/) and navigate to the "Download" section. Download the SFML source code.

2. **Extract SFML**: Extract the downloaded SFML archive to a directory of your choice. This directory will be referred to as your "SFML source directory."

3. **Build SFML**: Open a terminal, navigate to your SFML source directory, and use the following commands to build and install SFML:

```
mkdir build
cd build
cmake ..
make
sudo make install
```

This will build SFML and install it on your system.

4.3.3 Creating Your First SFML Project

With SFML set up on your Linux system, you can create your first SFML project. Here's a simple example of a Hello World program using SFML:

```cpp
#include <SFML/Graphics.hpp>

int main() {
    sf::RenderWindow window(sf::VideoMode(800, 600), "SFML Hello World");

    while (window.isOpen()) {
        sf::Event event;
        while (window.pollEvent(event)) {
            if (event.type == sf::Event::Closed) {
                window.close();
            }
        }

        window.clear();
        // Draw your graphics here
        window.display();
    }

    return 0;
}
```

This minimal SFML program creates a window, handles the close event, clears the window, and displays it. You can start adding your graphics, handling input, and building your games or applications on Linux using SFML.

In the next section, we'll discuss choosing the right code editor or integrated development environment (IDE) for your SFML projects and configuring it for optimal development on various platforms.

4.4 Choosing the Right Code Editor or IDE

When developing with SFML, choosing the right code editor or integrated development environment (IDE) is crucial for a smooth development experience. Your choice may depend on your personal preferences and the platform you're using. In this section, we'll discuss some popular code editors and IDEs for SFML development and provide guidance on configuring them for optimal development.

4.4.1 Visual Studio Code (VSCode)

Visual Studio Code is a free, open-source code editor that supports a wide range of programming languages and extensions, making it a versatile choice for SFML development. Here's how to set up Visual Studio Code for SFML:

1. **Install Visual Studio Code**: Download and install Visual Studio Code from the official website (https://code.visualstudio.com/).

2. **Install the C/C++ Extension**: Open VSCode and go to the Extensions view by clicking the square icon on the left sidebar. Search for the "C/C++" extension by Microsoft and install it.

3. **Configure Include and Library Directories**: In your SFML project, you need to configure the include and library directories for IntelliSense to work correctly. You can do this by creating a .vscode folder in your project directory and adding a c_cpp_properties.json file. Here's an example configuration for SFML:

```
{
    "configurations": [
        {
            "name": "Linux",
            "includePath": [
                "${workspaceFolder}/**",
                "/path/to/SFML/include" // Replace with your SFML include directory
            ],
            "defines": [],
            "compilerPath": "/usr/bin/g++", // Path to your C++ compiler
            "cStandard": "c11",
            "cppStandard": "c++17",
            "intelliSenseMode": "gcc-x64"
        },
        {
            "name": "Mac",
            "includePath": [
                "${workspaceFolder}/**",
                "/path/to/SFML/include" // Replace with your SFML include directory
```

```
        ],
        "defines": [],
        "compilerPath": "/usr/bin/g++", // Path to your C++ compiler
        "cStandard": "c11",
        "cppStandard": "c++17",
        "intelliSenseMode": "gcc-x64"
    },
    {
        "name": "Windows",
        "includePath": [
            "${workspaceFolder}/**",
            "C:/path/to/SFML/include" // Replace with your SFML include d
irectory on Windows
        ],
        "defines": [],
        "compilerPath": "C:/path/to/mingw/bin/g++.exe", // Path to your M
inGW g++ compiler on Windows
        "cStandard": "c11",
        "cppStandard": "c++17",
        "intelliSenseMode": "gcc-x64"
    }
    ],
    "version": 4
}
```

This configuration specifies include paths, compiler paths, and standards for different platforms (Linux, Mac, and Windows). Adjust the paths to match your SFML installation and compiler setup.

4. **Install SFML**: Ensure that you have SFML installed on your system, as discussed in previous sections.

5. **Create and Build Your Project**: Create a new project directory, write your SFML code, and use the terminal integrated into VSCode to build and run your project.

4.4.2 CLion

CLion is a commercial cross-platform IDE by JetBrains that offers excellent C++ support, making it a robust choice for SFML development. Here's how to set up CLion for SFML:

1. **Install CLion**: Download and install CLion from the JetBrains website (https://www.jetbrains.com/clion/).

2. **Create a New Project**: Start CLion and create a new C++ project.

3. **Configure CMakeLists.txt**: SFML projects typically use CMake for building. Create a CMakeLists.txt file in your project directory with the following content:

```
cmake_minimum_required(VERSION 3.0)
project(SFMLProject)
```

```
set(CMAKE_CXX_STANDARD 17)

# Locate SFML
find_package(SFML 2.5 COMPONENTS graphics audio REQUIRED)

add_executable(SFMLProject main.cpp)

# Link SFML libraries to your project
target_link_libraries(SFMLProject sfml-graphics sfml-audio)
```

This CMakeLists.txt file sets the C++ standard, finds SFML, and links the necessary SFML libraries to your project.

4. **Create and Build Your Project**: Write your SFML code in CLion, and use the built-in CMake integration to build and run your project.

4.4.3 Qt Creator

Qt Creator is an open-source IDE primarily designed for Qt development but can be used for C++ development, including SFML. Here's how to set up Qt Creator for SFML:

1. **Install Qt Creator**: Download and install Qt Creator from the Qt website (https://www.qt.io/download).

2. **Create a New Project**: Start Qt Creator and create a new C++ project.

3. **Configure Your Project**: In your project settings, add the include and library directories for SFML. Under "Projects" > "Build & Run," you can set the include and library paths for your project.

4. **Link SFML Libraries**: In your project settings, go to "Projects" > "Build & Run" > "Build" > "Build Steps." In the "Make" field, add the flags to link SFML libraries. For example, to link SFML Graphics and Audio libraries, you can add:

```
-lsfml-graphics -lsfml-audio
```

5. **Create and Build Your Project**: Write your SFML code in Qt Creator and use the built-in build system to compile and run your project.

These are just a few examples of code editors and IDEs you can use for SFML development. Ultimately, the choice of IDE depends on your preferences and your

4.5 Configuring Your Development Environment

Configuring your development environment for SFML is an essential step to ensure a smooth and efficient workflow. In this section, we'll discuss various aspects of configuring your development environment, including code formatting, version control, and build automation.

4.5.1 Code Formatting

Consistent code formatting is crucial for maintaining clean and readable code, especially in collaborative projects. Many code editors and IDEs offer built-in or third-party code formatting tools that can help you achieve a consistent coding style. Here are some common tools and tips for code formatting in SFML projects:

- **Editor/IDE Settings**: Most code editors and IDEs allow you to configure code formatting settings. You can specify your preferred coding style, indentation, and code formatting rules.

- **EditorConfig**: EditorConfig (https://editorconfig.org/) is a widely used standard for defining coding styles in a project. You can create an `.editorconfig` file in your SFML project directory to specify code formatting rules that will be respected by various code editors and IDEs.

- **ClangFormat**: ClangFormat (https://clang.llvm.org/docs/ClangFormat.html) is a powerful code formatting tool that can automatically format your code according to predefined style rules. You can create a `.clang-format` file in your project directory to configure ClangFormat.

- **Pre-Commit Hooks**: Consider setting up pre-commit hooks that automatically format your code before each commit. Tools like Git hooks or pre-commit (https://pre-commit.com/) can be used for this purpose.

- **Coding Guidelines**: Establish coding guidelines for your SFML project and document them in a style guide. This guide can include rules for naming conventions, indentation, comments, and other coding practices.

4.5.2 Version Control with Git

Version control is essential for tracking changes to your SFML project, collaborating with team members, and managing different versions of your code. Git is one of the most widely used version control systems and is well-suited for SFML development. Here are some steps to configure version control for your SFML project:

- **Initialize a Git Repository**: If your project is not already under version control, you can initialize a Git repository in your project directory using the following command:

```
git init
```

- **Create a .gitignore File**: Create a `.gitignore` file in your project directory to specify which files and directories should be excluded from version control. For SFML projects, you can ignore build artifacts, temporary files, and other generated files. Here's a sample `.gitignore` for an SFML project:

```
# Build artifacts
/build/
```

```
# macOS system files
.DS_Store

# Compiled object files
*.o

# Compiled dynamic libraries
*.so
*.dylib

# Compiled executables
*.out
```

- **Commit Your Changes**: Use Git to commit your changes regularly. Each commit should represent a meaningful and atomic change to your codebase. Remember to write descriptive commit messages to document the purpose of each commit.

- **Collaborate on GitHub/Bitbucket**: If you're working on a team or want to share your SFML project with others, consider using platforms like GitHub or Bitbucket to host your Git repository. These platforms provide collaboration features, issue tracking, and version control hosting.

- **Branching**: Utilize Git branches to work on different features or bug fixes concurrently. Create feature branches, make changes, and merge them back into the main branch (usually `master` or `main`) when they are ready.

4.5.3 Build Automation with CMake

CMake is a popular build automation tool that simplifies the process of compiling and building SFML projects on different platforms. It generates platform-specific build files (e.g., Makefiles, Visual Studio project files) based on a CMake configuration file. Here's how to configure CMake for your SFML project:

- **CMakeLists.txt**: Create a `CMakeLists.txt` file in your project directory. This file defines how your project should be built, including dependencies and compiler options. Refer to the SFML documentation and CMake documentation for guidance on configuring your `CMakeLists.txt`.

- **Out-of-Source Builds**: Consider using out-of-source builds, where the build files and generated binaries are stored in a separate directory from your source code. This keeps your source directory clean and allows for easy cleanup.

- **CMake GUI**: CMake provides a graphical user interface (CMake GUI) that can help you configure your project more easily, especially if you have complex dependencies or want to set specific options.

- **Cross-Platform Support**: CMake is designed to be cross-platform, making it suitable for SFML projects on Windows, macOS, and Linux. Your CMakeLists.txt can include platform-specific logic to handle different environments.

- **Building with CMake**: Use CMake to generate build files based on your CMakeLists.txt configuration. For example, you can run the following commands in your project directory:

```
mkdir build
cd build
cmake ..
make
```

These steps will configure your development environment for SFML, ensuring that your code is formatted consistently, version-controlled with Git, and built using CMake. With a well-configured development environment, you can focus on coding and creating engaging SFML games and applications.

Chapter 5: Managing Projects with CMake

CMake is a powerful cross-platform build system and project management tool that is commonly used in SFML game development. In this chapter, we'll delve into how to manage your SFML projects efficiently using CMake. You'll learn how to create CMakeLists.txt files, build projects, manage dependencies, and achieve cross-platform compatibility.

5.1 Introduction to CMake

CMake is an open-source tool that automates the process of building, testing, and packaging software projects. It generates platform-specific build files (e.g., Makefiles, Visual Studio project files) from a human-readable configuration file (CMakeLists.txt). Using CMake offers several benefits for SFML projects:

- **Cross-Platform Compatibility**: CMake is designed to work seamlessly on various platforms, including Windows, macOS, and Linux. This makes it an excellent choice for developing cross-platform SFML applications.

- **Simplified Build Process**: CMake simplifies the build process by providing a unified interface to configure, build, and install your project. It abstracts platform-specific details, making it easier to maintain and share your code.

- **Dependency Management**: CMake allows you to specify and manage dependencies, including libraries like SFML. It helps ensure that your project can find and link to the required libraries, even on different systems.

- **Out-of-Source Builds**: CMake encourages out-of-source builds, where build files and binaries are generated in a separate directory from the source code. This keeps your source directory clean and allows for multiple build configurations.

- **Integration with IDEs**: CMake integrates with popular integrated development environments (IDEs) like Visual Studio, CLion, and Qt Creator, making it easier to work with SFML in these environments.

- **Custom Configuration**: You can define custom configuration options in your CMakeLists.txt file, enabling fine-grained control over your build process. This is especially useful for specifying compiler flags, build types, and project-specific settings.

Here's a basic example of a CMakeLists.txt file for an SFML project:

```
cmake_minimum_required(VERSION 3.0)
project(SFMLProject)

# Find SFML
find_package(SFML 2.5 COMPONENTS graphics audio REQUIRED)
```

```
# Define the executable
add_executable(SFMLProject main.cpp)

# Link SFML libraries to your project
target_link_libraries(SFMLProject sfml-graphics sfml-audio)
```

In this simple example, CMake is used to find the SFML library, define the executable, and link the necessary SFML libraries to the project. You can customize this file to suit your project's specific requirements.

In the following sections, we'll explore CMake in more detail, discussing how to create CMakeLists.txt files, build your SFML projects, manage dependencies, and ensure cross-platform compatibility.

5.2 Creating CMakeLists.txt Files

In SFML game development, CMakeLists.txt files play a pivotal role in configuring and building your projects. These files define how your project should be built, specify dependencies, and set various build options. In this section, we'll dive into creating CMakeLists.txt files for your SFML projects and understanding their structure.

Basic Structure of a CMakeLists.txt File

A CMakeLists.txt file consists of commands and directives that instruct CMake on how to build your project. Here's a basic structure for an SFML project's CMakeLists.txt file:

```
cmake_minimum_required(VERSION 3.0)
project(SFMLProject)

# Set C++ standard (optional)
set(CMAKE_CXX_STANDARD 17)

# Find SFML
find_package(SFML 2.5 COMPONENTS graphics audio REQUIRED)

# Define the executable
add_executable(SFMLProject main.cpp)

# Link SFML libraries to your project
target_link_libraries(SFMLProject sfml-graphics sfml-audio)
```

Let's break down the components of this CMakeLists.txt file:

- cmake_minimum_required(VERSION 3.0): This line specifies the minimum required CMake version. Make sure you specify an appropriate version for your project.

- `project(SFMLProject)`: This line defines the project's name, which you can customize.

- `set(CMAKE_CXX_STANDARD 17)`: (Optional) If you want to set a specific C++ standard, you can use this command. In this example, C++17 is specified, but you can choose a different standard if needed.

- `find_package(SFML 2.5 COMPONENTS graphics audio REQUIRED)`: This command instructs CMake to find the SFML library, specifically the graphics and audio components. The `REQUIRED` keyword ensures that SFML is found; otherwise, it will generate an error.

- `add_executable(SFMLProject main.cpp)`: This line defines the executable that will be generated. The `SFMLProject` is the name of the executable, and `main.cpp` is the source file containing your application's entry point.

- `target_link_libraries(SFMLProject sfml-graphics sfml-audio)`: This command specifies the libraries that should be linked to your project. Here, we link the SFML graphics and audio libraries to the `SFMLProject` executable.

Customizing CMake Configuration

You can customize your CMake configuration to meet the specific needs of your SFML project. Some common customizations include:

- **Adding More Source Files**: If your project consists of multiple source files, list them after `main.cpp` in the `add_executable` command.

- **Specifying Compiler Flags**: Use the `target_compile_options` command to specify compiler flags and options for your project. For example, you can set optimization flags, enable or disable warnings, or define preprocessor macros.

- **Including External Libraries**: If your project relies on external libraries other than SFML, you can use the `find_package` command to locate and include them in your build.

- **Organizing Source Files into Directories**: If your project has a complex directory structure, you can use CMake to organize source files into directories and specify dependencies between them.

- **Configuring Build Types**: You can define different build types (e.g., Debug, Release) and set specific compiler options, flags, and build directories for each type.

- **Enabling Features**: Use CMake options to enable or disable specific features in your project. For instance, you can create an option to toggle debug logging or other runtime behaviors.

Customizing your CMake configuration allows you to tailor it to the requirements of your SFML project. As your project evolves, you can modify the CMakeLists.txt file to accommodate changes and additions. This flexibility is valuable for maintaining complex projects and ensuring smooth builds across different platforms.

5.3 Building Projects with CMake

Building SFML projects using CMake is a crucial step in the development process. CMake simplifies the build process, generating platform-specific build files from your CMakeLists.txt configuration. In this section, we'll explore how to use CMake to build your SFML projects, including common commands and best practices.

Running CMake

To build your SFML project with CMake, follow these steps:

1. **Create a Build Directory**: It's recommended to create a separate build directory to keep your source directory clean. This is known as an "out-of-source" build. For example, if your project is in a directory called "SFMLProject," you can create a build directory like this:

```
mkdir build
cd build
```

2. **Run CMake**: Inside the build directory, run CMake with the path to your project's source directory. This command generates the necessary build files based on your CMakeLists.txt configuration.

```
cmake ..
```

If you have specific build requirements, you can pass additional options to CMake. For example, to build in Debug mode, you can use:

```
cmake -DCMAKE_BUILD_TYPE=Debug ..
```

3. **Build Your Project**: After running CMake, you can build your project using platform-specific build tools. For example, on Unix-based systems, you can use "make":

```
make
```

On Windows, you might use Visual Studio or another IDE that CMake supports.

Configuring Build Types

CMake allows you to specify different build types, such as Debug, Release, or custom configurations. The build type determines compiler flags, optimization levels, and other build options. You can set the build type when running CMake using the -DCMAKE_BUILD_TYPE option.

For example, to build a Debug version:

```
cmake -DCMAKE_BUILD_TYPE=Debug ..
```

To build a Release version with optimizations:

```
cmake -DCMAKE_BUILD_TYPE=Release ..
```

It's a good practice to create both Debug and Release builds for your SFML projects. Debug builds are useful for development and debugging, while Release builds are optimized for performance.

Building on Different Platforms

CMake is designed for cross-platform development, so it can generate build files for various platforms. When you run CMake on different platforms, it automatically adapts to the platform's build tools and conventions.

For example, on Windows, CMake might generate Visual Studio project files, while on Linux, it generates Makefiles. This cross-platform capability makes it easier to share your SFML projects with others who use different operating systems.

Using IDEs with CMake

Many integrated development environments (IDEs) support CMake integration, making it even easier to build and work on your SFML projects. IDEs like Visual Studio, CLion, and Qt Creator can open CMake-based projects directly and provide a familiar development environment.

To use an IDE with CMake, you typically perform the following steps:

1. Create a build directory (if you haven't already).

2. Run CMake from within the build directory to generate the appropriate project files for your chosen IDE. For example:

   ```
   cmake -G "Visual Studio 16 2019" ..
   ```

   Replace "Visual Studio 16 2019" with the generator name appropriate for your IDE.

3. Open the generated project files in your IDE. The IDE will recognize the CMake configuration and project structure.

4. Build and run your project from within the IDE.

Using an IDE with CMake can streamline your development workflow and provide features like code navigation, debugging, and version control integration.

With your CMakeLists.txt configuration in place and the build files generated, you can build your SFML project using the appropriate build tools for your platform. The build process compiles your source code and links it with the SFML library and any other dependencies you've specified.

Remember to select the correct build type (Debug or Release) depending on your needs. Debug builds are suitable for development and debugging, while Release builds optimize your code for performance.

In summary, CMake is a versatile tool for building SFML projects across different platforms. It simplifies the build process, allows you to configure different build types, and integrates with various IDEs. By following the steps outlined in this section, you can efficiently build and develop your SFML applications.

5.4 Managing Dependencies with CMake

Managing dependencies is a crucial aspect of SFML game development, and CMake provides a powerful mechanism for handling these dependencies seamlessly. In this section, we'll explore how to manage dependencies using CMake, including adding external libraries and finding package dependencies.

Adding External Libraries

SFML itself is a library, but your SFML project might depend on other libraries or frameworks to accomplish specific tasks. CMake simplifies the process of adding external libraries to your project. Here are the steps to do so:

1. **Locate the Library**: First, ensure that the external library is installed on your system or available as a downloadable package. You'll need the library's include files (headers) and compiled binaries.

2. **Create a CMake Configuration File (Optional)**: If the library provides a CMake configuration file (often named `FindLibraryName.cmake`), you can use it to simplify the integration process. These configuration files define how CMake should find and use the library.

3. **Modify Your CMakeLists.txt**: In your project's CMakeLists.txt file, you can use the `find_package` command to locate the external library. For example, if you have a library named "MyLibrary," you might do the following:

   ```
   find_package(MyLibrary REQUIRED)
   ```

4. **Link the Library**: After finding the library, you should link it to your project using the `target_link_libraries` command:

```
target_link_libraries(SFMLProject MyLibrary)
```

5. **Include Headers**: Ensure that you include the necessary headers from the external library in your source code.

CMake provides a versatile mechanism for finding package dependencies, including libraries, tools, and frameworks, that are commonly used in C++ projects. This mechanism is especially helpful for managing dependencies in a cross-platform manner. To find package dependencies, follow these steps:

1. **Specify Required Packages**: In your CMakeLists.txt file, specify the required package dependencies using the find_package command. You can specify multiple packages if needed:

```
find_package(SFML 2.5 COMPONENTS graphics audio REQUIRED)
find_package(OpenGL REQUIRED)
```

Here, we're specifying both SFML and OpenGL as required dependencies.

2. **Check for Package Availability**: After specifying the packages, CMake will check if they are available on the system. If any required packages are missing, CMake will generate an error.

3. **Use Found Packages**: If CMake finds the required packages, you can use the found package variables to configure your project. For example, you might enable certain features or set compiler flags based on the presence of specific packages.

```
if(SFML_FOUND)
    target_link_libraries(SFMLProject sfml-graphics sfml-audio)
endif()
```

```
if(OpenGL_FOUND)
    target_link_libraries(SFMLProject ${OPENGL_LIBRARIES})
endif()
```

4. **Include Headers**: Make sure to include the headers from the packages you use in your source code.

Handling Non-CMake Dependencies

In some cases, you might need to work with dependencies that don't provide CMake configuration files. For such dependencies, you can use CMake's ExternalProject module, which allows you to download, build, and integrate external projects into your CMake-based project. While this approach is more complex, it provides a way to manage non-CMake dependencies.

To use ExternalProject, you'll typically create a custom CMake target that invokes ExternalProject_Add with the necessary build instructions for the external dependency.

Package managers like Conan and vcpkg can also simplify dependency management in CMake-based projects. These package managers can automatically download, build, and integrate external libraries into your project, making it easier to handle complex dependencies.

Conan, for example, allows you to define your project's dependencies in a configuration file and fetch them as part of your build process. vcpkg offers precompiled binary packages for many popular libraries, which can be easily integrated into your CMake-based project.

In summary, CMake provides a flexible and powerful way to manage dependencies in your SFML projects. Whether you're dealing with external libraries, package dependencies, or non-CMake dependencies, CMake offers the tools and commands needed to seamlessly integrate and manage these dependencies in a cross-platform manner.

5.5 Cross-Platform Compatibility with CMake

One of the significant advantages of using CMake in SFML game development is its ability to ensure cross-platform compatibility. CMake abstracts the build process and generates platform-specific build files, allowing you to write your SFML code once and compile it on various operating systems without modification. In this section, we'll explore best practices for achieving cross-platform compatibility with CMake.

Write Portable C++ Code

The foundation of cross-platform compatibility is writing portable C++ code. This means avoiding platform-specific features and adhering to C++ standards. Here are some tips for writing portable code in your SFML projects:

- **Use Cross-Platform Libraries**: Whenever possible, rely on cross-platform libraries like SFML for handling platform-specific tasks such as window management, input handling, and multimedia.

- **Avoid Non-Standard Features**: Avoid using non-standard or platform-specific C++ features or libraries. Stick to the C++ standard library and features provided by SFML.

- **Handle Platform Differences**: If you encounter platform-specific differences in behavior, create platform-specific code branches using preprocessor directives (#ifdef, #endif) and macros (#define). For example, you might need to handle file path differences between Windows and Unix-like systems.

Leverage CMake's Cross-Platform Features

CMake itself is a cross-platform tool, and it excels at generating build files for different platforms. Here's how to leverage CMake for cross-platform compatibility:

- **Use CMake Variables**: CMake defines platform-specific variables that you can use in your CMakeLists.txt files. For example, `CMAKE_SYSTEM_NAME` holds the name of the current operating system (e.g., "Windows," "Linux," "Darwin" for macOS). You can conditionally set options and variables based on the target platform.

```
if (CMAKE_SYSTEM_NAME STREQUAL "Windows")
    # Windows-specific configuration
elseif (CMAKE_SYSTEM_NAME STREQUAL "Linux")
    # Linux-specific configuration
elseif (CMAKE_SYSTEM_NAME STREQUAL "Darwin")
    # macOS-specific configuration
endif()
```

- **Cross-Compile**: CMake allows cross-compilation, which means you can build for a different target architecture or platform than the one you're currently using. This is useful for embedded systems or cross-compiling for mobile platforms.

- **Handle Library Naming Conventions**: Different platforms have different naming conventions for shared libraries (DLLs on Windows, SO files on Linux, DYLIB files on macOS). CMake helps you manage these differences with variables like `CMAKE_SHARED_LIBRARY_PREFIX` and `CMAKE_SHARED_LIBRARY_SUFFIX`.

Use CMake's Built-In Features

CMake provides built-in features and functions that help ensure cross-platform compatibility:

- **File Path Handling**: CMake offers cross-platform functions for handling file paths. Use `file(TO_CMAKE_PATH)` to convert file paths to the platform's format, ensuring compatibility.

- **Compiler Flags and Options**: Use CMake to set compiler flags and options that are appropriate for the target platform. For example, you can set optimization levels, specify the target architecture, and enable platform-specific features.

- **Compiler Checks**: CMake's `check_function_exists`, `check_symbol_exists`, and similar functions help you detect the availability of functions and symbols in a cross-platform manner. You can use these checks to conditionally enable or disable features based on platform support.

Continuous Integration (CI) and Testing

To ensure cross-platform compatibility, set up a CI system that builds and tests your SFML project on various platforms. Popular CI services like Travis CI, GitHub Actions, and Jenkins allow you to automate this process. Regularly testing on different platforms helps catch and fix compatibility issues early in development.

In summary, achieving cross-platform compatibility with CMake in SFML game development involves writing portable code, leveraging CMake's cross-platform features, using built-in functions for file path handling and compiler checks, and implementing CI and testing procedures. By following these best practices, you can create SFML games that run smoothly on Windows, Linux, macOS, and other platforms.

Chapter 6: Creating the Classic Game of Pong

6.1 Designing the Pong Game

In this section, we'll dive into the design process of creating the classic game of Pong using SFML. Pong is a simple yet iconic game that serves as an excellent starting point for learning game development with SFML.

Game Concept

Pong is a two-player game where each player controls a paddle. The objective is to score points by bouncing a ball past the opponent's paddle. The game continues until one player reaches a specified score or until the players decide to end it.

Game Elements

To create Pong, we'll need the following game elements:

1. **Paddles**: Two paddles, one for each player, that can move vertically within their respective halves of the screen. Players use the paddles to hit the ball.

2. **Ball**: A ball that bounces around the screen. The ball's direction changes when it hits a paddle or the top or bottom edges of the screen.

3. **Score**: A scoring system to keep track of each player's score. The game should display the current score on the screen.

4. **Game Logic**: Logic to control the movement of the paddles and the ball. This includes handling collisions, scoring points, and determining when the game ends.

Game Flow

The game flow can be divided into the following steps:

1. **Initialization**: Set up the game window, load textures for paddles and the ball, initialize scores, and set the initial position and velocity of the ball.

2. **Input Handling**: Continuously listen for player input to move the paddles up and down.

3. **Update**: Update the position of the ball based on its velocity. Check for collisions with paddles or screen edges and update the score accordingly.

4. **Rendering**: Draw the paddles, ball, and scores on the game window to display the game's current state.

5. **Game Over**: When one player reaches the winning score or decides to end the game, display the winner, and allow the option to restart.

- **Graphics**: Decide on the visual style of the game. You can use simple shapes for paddles and the ball or create custom graphics.

- **Sound**: Consider adding sound effects for ball bounces and scoring events to enhance the gaming experience.

- **Difficulty**: You can adjust the game's difficulty by changing the ball's speed, paddle size, or other factors.

- **Multiplayer**: Pong can be played in multiplayer mode, where two human players compete, or in single-player mode against an AI opponent.

In the following sections, we'll implement each aspect of the Pong game, starting with the creation of game objects and handling their movement and collision.

6.2 Implementing Game Objects

In this section, we'll delve into the implementation of game objects for our Pong game. Game objects are the fundamental entities in a game, and for Pong, we primarily have two types: paddles and the ball. We'll create classes for these game objects, define their properties, and handle their movement and rendering.

Creating a Paddle Class

We'll begin by creating a `Paddle` class to represent the paddles controlled by the players. Each paddle should have attributes like position, size, speed, and a method to move the paddle up or down. Here's a simplified example of the `Paddle` class in C++:

```cpp
class Paddle {
public:
    Paddle(float startX, float startY, float width, float height, float speed
);

    void moveUp();
    void moveDown();
    void update(sf::Time deltaTime);
    void draw(sf::RenderWindow& window);

private:
    sf::RectangleShape shape;
    float speed;
};
```

In this class: - We initialize the `sf::RectangleShape` to represent the paddle's visual appearance. - The `moveUp` and `moveDown` methods change the position of the paddle to simulate its movement. - The `update` method can be used to update the paddle's logic, such as collision detection (we'll implement this later). - The `draw` method renders the paddle on the game window.

Next, we'll create a `Ball` class to represent the game ball. Like the `Paddle` class, the `Ball` class should have attributes such as position, size, velocity, and methods for updating and rendering the ball.

```
class Ball {
public:
    Ball(float startX, float startY, float radius, float speed);

    void update(sf::Time deltaTime);
    void draw(sf::RenderWindow& window);

    void resetPosition(); // Reset the ball's position for a new round.
    void launch(); // Launch the ball at the beginning of a round.

private:
    sf::CircleShape shape;
    sf::Vector2f velocity;
};
```

In this class: - We use `sf::CircleShape` to represent the ball's visual appearance. - The `update` method moves the ball based on its velocity. - The `draw` method renders the ball. - `resetPosition` and `launch` methods help with starting a new round of the game.

Initializing and Managing Game Objects

In the main game loop, you would create instances of the `Paddle` and `Ball` classes and manage their updates and rendering. You'd also handle player input to control the paddles.

Here's a simplified example of managing game objects in the game loop:

```
Paddle player1(/* initial parameters */);
Paddle player2(/* initial parameters */);
Ball ball(/* initial parameters */);

while (window.isOpen()) {
    sf::Event event;
    while (window.pollEvent(event)) {
        // Handle user input here.
    }

    // Update game objects.
    player1.update(deltaTime);
    player2.update(deltaTime);
    ball.update(deltaTime);
```

```
// Collision detection and game logic will be implemented later.

// Clear the window.
window.clear();

// Draw game objects.
player1.draw(window);
player2.draw(window);
ball.draw(window);

// Display the frame.
window.display();
}
```

In this code, we create instances of the Paddle and Ball classes and update and draw them in the game loop. However, we haven't implemented collision detection or game logic yet. These aspects will be covered in later sections as we build the complete Pong game.

6.3 Handling Collision Detection

In this section, we'll focus on implementing collision detection for our Pong game. Collision detection is a critical aspect of any game and is essential for determining when game objects interact with each other. In Pong, we need to detect collisions between the ball and the paddles and between the ball and the screen boundaries.

Collision Detection Basics

1. Ball-Paddle Collision

To detect collisions between the ball and the paddles, we can use simple bounding box collision. We compare the position and size of the ball and the paddles to check if they overlap. If they do, a collision has occurred.

Here's a simplified example of how we can detect a collision between the ball and a paddle in the Ball class:

```
bool Ball::checkPaddleCollision(const Paddle& paddle) {
    // Get the bounding boxes of the ball and the paddle.
    sf::FloatRect ballBounds = shape.getGlobalBounds();
    sf::FloatRect paddleBounds = paddle.getShape().getGlobalBounds();

    // Check for collision.
    if (ballBounds.intersects(paddleBounds)) {
        // Handle collision here.
        return true;
    }
    return false;
}
```

2. Ball-Screen Boundary Collision

To detect collisions between the ball and the screen boundaries (top and bottom), we need to compare the ball's position and size with the screen's dimensions. If the ball goes beyond the screen boundaries, it has collided with the screen.

Here's a simplified example of how we can detect collisions with the screen boundaries in the Ball class:

```cpp
bool Ball::checkScreenBoundaryCollision(float screenHeight) {
    // Get the current position of the ball.
    sf::Vector2f position = shape.getPosition();

    // Check top boundary collision.
    if (position.y - shape.getRadius() < 0) {
        // Handle collision with the top boundary.
        return true;
    }

    // Check bottom boundary collision.
    if (position.y + shape.getRadius() > screenHeight) {
        // Handle collision with the bottom boundary.
        return true;
    }

    return false;
}
```

Handling Collisions

In the game loop, you would continuously check for collisions between the ball and the paddles and between the ball and the screen boundaries. If a collision is detected, you can change the direction of the ball's velocity accordingly.

Here's a simplified example of handling collisions in the game loop:

```cpp
// Check for collisions with paddles.
if (ball.checkPaddleCollision(player1) || ball.checkPaddleCollision(player2))
{
    // Handle paddle collision by changing the ball's direction.
    ball.reverseXVelocity();
}

// Check for collisions with screen boundaries.
if (ball.checkScreenBoundaryCollision(screenHeight)) {
    // Handle screen boundary collision by reversing the ball's Y velocity.
    ball.reverseYVelocity();
}
```

In this code, we call the collision detection methods for both paddles and screen boundaries. If a collision is detected, we update the ball's velocity to simulate the bounce effect.

As we continue building the Pong game, we'll refine the collision handling and add scoring logic and game flow to create a fully functional game.

6.4 Managing Game States

In this section, we'll explore how to manage different game states within our Pong game. Game states allow us to switch between various phases of the game, such as the main menu, gameplay, and game over screens. For Pong, we'll focus on three essential game states: start menu, gameplay, and game over.

Game State Design

1. Start Menu State

The start menu state is the initial state when the game starts. It typically displays the game title, instructions, and options to start a new game or quit.

```
enum class GameState {
    StartMenu,
    Gameplay,
    GameOver
};
```

2. Gameplay State

The gameplay state is where the actual game takes place. Players can control the paddles, and the ball moves around the screen. The gameplay state can also include scoring logic and conditions to determine when the game is over.

3. Game Over State

The game over state is displayed when the game ends. It shows the final score and provides options to restart the game or return to the start menu.

Implementing Game State Switching

To manage game states, we can use a state machine approach. We define a variable to keep track of the current game state, and in the game loop, we update and render different game objects based on the current state.

Here's a simplified example of how game state switching can be implemented:

```
GameState currentState = GameState::StartMenu;

while (window.isOpen()) {
```

```cpp
            sf::Event event;
            while (window.pollEvent(event)) {
                // Handle user input here based on the current state.
                switch (currentState) {
                    case GameState::StartMenu:
                        // Handle start menu input.
                        break;
                    case GameState::Gameplay:
                        // Handle gameplay input.
                        break;
                    case GameState::GameOver:
                        // Handle game over input.
                        break;
                }
            }

            // Update and render game objects based on the current state.
            switch (currentState) {
                case GameState::StartMenu:
                    // Update and render start menu objects.
                    break;
                case GameState::Gameplay:
                    // Update and render gameplay objects.
                    break;
                case GameState::GameOver:
                    // Update and render game over objects.
                    break;
            }

            // Check conditions for state transitions.
            switch (currentState) {
                case GameState::StartMenu:
                    // Check conditions to start the gameplay state.
                    if (/* Start button pressed */) {
                        currentState = GameState::Gameplay;
                        // Initialize gameplay here.
                    }
                    break;
                case GameState::Gameplay:
                    // Check conditions for game over state.
                    if (/* Game over condition met */) {
                        currentState = GameState::GameOver;
                        // Initialize game over screen here.
                    }
                    break;
                case GameState::GameOver:
                    // Check conditions to return to the start menu.
                    if (/* Return to menu button pressed */) {
                        currentState = GameState::StartMenu;
                        // Reset game here.
```

```
        }
        break;
    }

    // Clear, draw, and display as usual.
    // ...
}
```

In this example, we use a `GameState` enum to represent different game states. We handle user input, update game objects, and check conditions for state transitions based on the current state. Depending on the state, we render different objects and perform specific actions.

By implementing game state management, we can create a structured and user-friendly gaming experience in our Pong game.

6.5 Adding Game Logic and Score

In this section, we'll dive into the implementation of game logic and scoring for our Pong game. Game logic is crucial for determining when a point is scored, managing game rounds, and declaring a winner. We'll also keep track of player scores and display them on the screen.

Scoring System

In Pong, scoring is relatively straightforward. When one player fails to return the ball, the opposing player scores a point. The game typically has a set number of rounds, and the player with the most points at the end wins.

We can represent the player scores using variables:

```
int player1Score = 0;
int player2Score = 0;
```

Scoring Logic

In the game loop, we need to implement scoring logic to detect when a point is scored. When the ball goes past one of the paddles and reaches the screen boundary, we increment the opposing player's score.

Here's a simplified example of scoring logic:

```
// Check for collisions with screen boundaries.
if (ball.checkScreenBoundaryCollision(screenHeight)) {
    if (ball.getPosition().x < 0) {
        // Player 2 scores a point.
        player2Score++;
    } else {
        // Player 1 scores a point.
```

```
        player1Score++;
    }

    // Reset the ball position and velocity for a new round.
    ball.resetPosition();
    ball.launch();
}
```

Round Management

In Pong, the game is played in rounds. Each round starts with the ball launching from the center of the screen towards one of the players. To manage rounds, we can use a variable that keeps track of the current round and a variable to determine which player serves the ball.

```
int currentRound = 0;
int servingPlayer = 1; // Player 1 serves first in most cases.

// ...

// Inside the game loop, check for a new round.
if (ball.checkScreenBoundaryCollision(screenHeight)) {
    // Increment the round counter.
    currentRound++;

    // Determine the serving player for the next round.
    servingPlayer = (currentRound % 2 == 0) ? 1 : 2;

    // Reset the ball position and velocity for a new round.
    ball.resetPosition();

    // Launch the ball from the serving player.
    if (servingPlayer == 1) {
        ball.launchRight(); // Ball moves to the right.
    } else {
        ball.launchLeft(); // Ball moves to the left.
    }
}
```

Displaying Scores

To display the player scores on the screen, you can use SFML's text rendering capabilities. Create two sf::Text objects for player 1 and player 2 scores, update them with the current scores in each frame, and draw them to the screen.

```
sf::Font font;
font.loadFromFile("font.ttf"); // Load a font for text rendering.

sf::Text player1ScoreText;
sf::Text player2ScoreText;
```

```cpp
player1ScoreText.setFont(font);
player2ScoreText.setFont(font);

// Set font size, color, position, etc.

// Inside the game loop, update the score text:
player1ScoreText.setString("Player 1: " + std::to_string(player1Score));
player2ScoreText.setString("Player 2: " + std::to_string(player2Score));

// Draw the score text on the screen.
window.draw(player1ScoreText);
window.draw(player2ScoreText);
```

By implementing scoring logic, round management, and displaying scores, we make our Pong game more engaging and competitive. Players can now keep track of their performance and compete to reach a set winning score or round limit.

Chapter 7: Debugging and Testing

7.1 Debugging Techniques for Game Development

Debugging is a crucial part of game development. It involves the process of identifying and fixing errors, issues, and unexpected behaviors in your game's code. In this section, we will explore various debugging techniques and tools that can help you streamline your game development process and create more stable and enjoyable games.

Print Debugging

One of the simplest and most widely used debugging techniques is print debugging. It involves inserting print statements (or log statements) into your code to output variable values, messages, or markers at specific points in your code.

Here's a basic example of print debugging in C++ using the `std::cout` stream:

```cpp
int health = 100;
std::cout << "Health: " << health << std::endl;

// ...

// Print the value of a variable inside a loop.
for (int i = 0; i < 10; i++) {
    std::cout << "i: " << i << std::endl;
}
```

Print debugging can help you track the flow of your program, inspect variable values, and identify when and where issues occur. However, it can be cumbersome in large and complex codebases.

Using Breakpoints

Integrated Development Environments (IDEs) like Visual Studio, Visual Studio Code, and JetBrains' CLion provide powerful debugging tools, including breakpoints. Breakpoints allow you to pause the execution of your code at a specific line or function call, giving you the opportunity to inspect variables, step through code, and identify issues in real-time.

Here's how to set a breakpoint in Visual Studio Code:

1. Open your project in Visual Studio Code.
2. Navigate to the line where you want to set a breakpoint.
3. Click on the left margin of the code editor, next to the line number. A red dot will appear, indicating a breakpoint.
4. Run your program in debugging mode.

When your code execution reaches the breakpoint, it will pause, and you can use debugging tools to inspect variables and step through the code.

Profiling and Performance Optimization

Performance is critical in game development, and profiling tools help you identify bottlenecks and optimize your code. Profilers measure various aspects of your program's performance, such as CPU usage, memory usage, and frame rendering times.

SFML provides a simple built-in profiler that you can use to measure the time taken by different parts of your game. Here's a basic example of how to use SFML's profiler:

```
sf::Clock clock;
// Code to profile here
float elapsedTime = clock.getElapsedTime().asSeconds();
std::cout << "Time taken: " << elapsedTime << " seconds" << std::endl;
```

Profiling tools outside of SFML, such as Valgrind and gprof, can provide more in-depth analysis of your program's performance.

Testing Your SFML Game

Testing is an essential part of game development to ensure that your game works as expected and that new changes or features do not introduce regressions. Automated testing frameworks like Google Test and Catch2 can be used to write unit tests for your game's components and functions.

Additionally, consider performing manual testing to play through your game and identify gameplay issues, glitches, and user experience problems.

In this section, we've explored some fundamental debugging techniques for game development, including print debugging, breakpoints, profiling, and testing. These techniques are essential for identifying and addressing issues in your game code and improving the overall quality of your game. As you continue to develop your game, you'll find that debugging becomes an integral part of your workflow, helping you create a polished and enjoyable gaming experience.

7.2 Using Breakpoints and Watches

In the world of game development, breakpoints and watches are invaluable tools for debugging and gaining insights into your code's behavior. They allow you to pause the execution of your program at specific points, inspect variables, and monitor expressions in real-time. In this section, we will delve into the usage of breakpoints and watches for debugging your SFML game.

Setting Breakpoints

Breakpoints are markers you place in your code to halt the program's execution when a specific line is reached. This pause gives you the opportunity to inspect variables, step through code, and understand what's happening at that moment.

To set a breakpoint in most integrated development environments (IDEs), you can usually click in the margin next to the line of code where you want to pause execution. A red dot or another indicator will appear to signify the breakpoint. When you run your program in debugging mode, it will stop at the breakpoint.

Here's a basic example using Visual Studio Code:

1. Open your SFML project in Visual Studio Code.
2. Navigate to the line in your code where you want to set a breakpoint.
3. Click in the left margin next to the line number. A red dot should appear, indicating a breakpoint is set.

Inspecting Variables

Once your program has paused at a breakpoint, you can inspect the values of variables at that moment. Most debugging environments provide a "Variables" or "Watch" panel where you can see the current state of variables.

For instance, if you're using Visual Studio Code with the C/C++ extension, you can view and interact with variables in the "Variables" panel. Clicking on a variable will show its current value, and you can modify variables' values during debugging, which can be helpful for testing different scenarios.

Using Watches

Watches are a powerful feature that allows you to monitor the values of specific variables or expressions continuously while your program runs. By setting up watches, you can keep an eye on critical values without manually inspecting them at breakpoints.

In Visual Studio Code, you can add a watch by following these steps:

1. While debugging, open the "Watch" panel.
2. Click the "Add Expression" button.
3. Enter the variable name or expression you want to watch.

Watches are particularly useful when you're interested in how a variable changes over time or when you need to track the value of a complex expression.

Conditional Breakpoints

Conditional breakpoints are breakpoints that only trigger when a specific condition is met. This condition can involve evaluating an expression or checking the value of a variable.

To set a conditional breakpoint, follow these steps:

1. Set a regular breakpoint at the desired line.
2. Right-click the breakpoint and choose "Edit Breakpoint."
3. Enter your condition in the provided field.

Conditional breakpoints are handy when you want to break execution only when certain conditions or states are reached, saving you time and allowing you to focus on specific scenarios.

Debugging Tips

- Use breakpoints strategically at points where you suspect issues may be occurring.
- Experiment with different conditional breakpoints to isolate specific problems.
- Combine watches with breakpoints to monitor variables of interest continuously.
- Familiarize yourself with your IDE's debugging features and keyboard shortcuts to improve your debugging efficiency.

In conclusion, breakpoints and watches are essential tools for debugging your SFML game. They allow you to control the execution flow, inspect variables, and gain insights into your code's behavior. Whether you're tracking down bugs or optimizing performance, these tools will help you create a more robust and enjoyable gaming experience.

7.3 Profiling and Performance Optimization

Performance optimization is a crucial aspect of game development, as it directly impacts the player's experience. In this section, we'll explore profiling techniques and tools to identify bottlenecks in your SFML game and optimize its performance.

Profiling Your Game

Profiling involves measuring various aspects of your game's performance, such as CPU usage, memory usage, and frame rendering times. Profilers provide insights into which parts of your code are consuming the most resources and can help you pinpoint areas that need improvement.

SFML provides a basic built-in profiler that you can use to measure the time taken by different parts of your game. Here's a simplified example of how to use SFML's profiler:

```cpp
sf::Clock clock;

// Code to profile here

float elapsedTime = clock.getElapsedTime().asSeconds();
std::cout << "Time taken: " << elapsedTime << " seconds" << std::endl;
```

While SFML's built-in profiler is useful for basic measurements, more advanced profiling tools can provide detailed reports and visualizations of your game's performance.

Using External Profiling Tools

External profiling tools like Valgrind, gprof, and Intel VTune can offer deeper insights into your game's performance characteristics. These tools can help you identify memory leaks, excessive CPU usage, and areas where optimizations are needed.

For example, Valgrind can detect memory-related issues, such as memory leaks and invalid memory access, by running your game in a specialized environment. Gprof, on the other hand, provides CPU usage and function call statistics to identify performance bottlenecks.

To use external profiling tools, you typically compile your game with special flags or settings to enable profiling. Then, you run your game under the profiler's control, and it generates reports and data that you can analyze.

Optimizing Your Game

Once you've identified performance bottlenecks using profiling tools, you can begin the process of optimization. Optimization involves making changes to your code to improve its performance while maintaining or even enhancing gameplay.

Common optimization techniques in game development include:

- **Algorithmic optimizations:** Review and improve the efficiency of your algorithms and data structures. Use more efficient sorting algorithms, optimize collision detection, and reduce redundant calculations.
- **Memory management:** Be mindful of memory usage and avoid memory leaks. Use smart pointers and release resources when they are no longer needed.
- **Parallelization:** Take advantage of multi-core processors by parallelizing tasks where possible. Multithreading can be used for tasks like physics simulations and rendering.
- **Asset optimization:** Compress textures and audio files, use texture atlases, and load assets asynchronously to reduce loading times and memory usage.
- **Render batching:** Combine multiple draw calls into a single batch to minimize the overhead of rendering operations.
- **Geometry culling:** Implement frustum culling and occlusion culling to avoid rendering objects that are not visible to the camera.

Remember that optimization is a continuous process, and it's essential to measure the impact of each optimization to ensure it delivers the expected performance improvements without introducing new issues.

Profiling and Optimizing Graphics

Graphics performance is a critical aspect of many games, and optimizing graphics rendering can have a significant impact on your game's frame rate. Consider the following graphics-related optimizations:

- **Level of detail (LOD):** Implement LOD techniques to render objects with varying levels of detail based on their distance from the camera.

- **Batching and instancing:** Combine multiple objects into a single batch for rendering, and use GPU instancing when applicable.
- **Shader optimization:** Optimize shaders to minimize unnecessary calculations and operations. Use shader profiling tools to identify performance bottlenecks in your shaders.

Profiling and Optimizing Physics

Physics simulations can also be resource-intensive. To optimize physics performance:

- **Collision culling:** Implement broad-phase and narrow-phase collision culling techniques to reduce the number of collision checks.
- **Simplify collision shapes:** Use simpler collision shapes (e.g., bounding boxes instead of complex polygons) when appropriate.
- **Multithreaded physics:** Parallelize physics calculations using multithreading to take advantage of multi-core processors.

Profiling and Optimizing Audio

Audio performance optimization is crucial for games with complex soundscapes:

- **Streaming audio:** Use audio streaming for long or dynamic audio tracks to reduce memory usage.
- **Sound mixing:** Optimize audio mixing algorithms to minimize CPU usage during sound playback.
- **Sound pooling:** Reuse sound instances to avoid the overhead of creating and destroying them frequently.

Profiling and Testing on Target Platforms

When optimizing your SFML game, it's essential to profile and test it on the target platforms where players will experience it. Different platforms may have varying hardware capabilities and performance characteristics, so optimizations that work well on one platform may not be as effective on another.

Profiling and Performance Targets

Setting clear performance targets for your game is essential. Define specific goals for frame rate, load times, and resource usage. Profiling tools can help you track your progress toward these goals and ensure that your game runs smoothly on a wide range of hardware configurations.

In summary, profiling and performance optimization are critical steps in the game development process. By using profiling tools, identifying bottlenecks, and

7.4 Testing Your SFML Game

Testing is a fundamental part of game development, ensuring that your game functions as intended and is free of critical bugs. In this section, we'll explore various aspects of testing your SFML game, from unit testing to playtesting.

Unit Testing

Unit testing is the practice of testing individual units or components of your code in isolation to ensure they work correctly. In game development, units can include functions, classes, or modules that make up your game's codebase.

To perform unit testing in C++ with SFML, you can use testing frameworks like Google Test or Catch2. These frameworks provide tools for writing and running tests and reporting results.

Here's a basic example using Google Test to test a function that calculates the score in a game:

```cpp
#include <gtest/gtest.h>
#include "game.h"

TEST(ScoreCalculationTest, CorrectScore) {
    Game game;
    game.AddPoints(50); // Add 50 points to the player's score
    ASSERT_EQ(game.GetScore(), 50); // Check if the score is 50
}

int main(int argc, char** argv) {
    ::testing::InitGoogleTest(&argc, argv);
    return RUN_ALL_TESTS();
}
```

Unit tests help catch regressions when you make changes to your code and ensure that existing functionality remains intact.

Integration Testing

Integration testing focuses on verifying that different parts of your game work together correctly. It tests interactions between components or systems rather than individual units. In game development, integration testing often involves testing how various game systems interact, such as physics, rendering, and input handling.

For example, you might test whether the collision detection system correctly triggers events when objects collide or if the player's input correctly influences the game's behavior.

Functional Testing

Functional testing examines whether your game functions correctly from a user's perspective. It involves testing scenarios that simulate how players will interact with your game. Functional testing can include:

- Verifying that game menus and user interfaces work as expected.
- Testing various game modes, levels, and progression.
- Ensuring that game mechanics, rules, and win/lose conditions are implemented correctly.
- Checking for usability and accessibility, such as controller support and colorblind-friendly options.

Functional testing often requires a dedicated testing team or thorough playtesting to cover a wide range of player experiences.

User Interface (UI) Testing

UI testing specifically focuses on testing the user interface elements of your game, such as menus, buttons, and HUD elements. It ensures that these elements are responsive, visually correct, and provide a smooth user experience.

UI testing can be automated using tools like Selenium or Appium for web-based games. For desktop games developed with SFML, you can create test scripts that simulate user interactions, such as clicking buttons and entering text, and verify the expected outcomes.

Playtesting

Playtesting is a critical form of testing that involves having actual players or testers play your game to provide feedback and identify issues. Playtesters can uncover gameplay imbalances, difficulty spikes, level design problems, and user experience issues that might not be apparent during development.

When conducting playtests, it's essential to gather feedback and observations from players and use their input to make improvements. Iterative playtesting throughout the development process can lead to a more enjoyable and polished game.

Performance Testing

Performance testing evaluates how your game performs under various conditions, such as different hardware configurations and network conditions for online games. It ensures that your game runs smoothly and meets performance targets, such as a stable frame rate and reasonable resource usage.

Tools like profiling and benchmarking can help identify performance bottlenecks and guide optimization efforts, as discussed in the previous section.

Regression Testing

Regression testing involves retesting your game after making changes or adding new features to ensure that existing functionality has not been inadvertently broken. Automated test suites can be valuable for regression testing, as they can quickly verify that previously tested features still work as expected.

Continuous Integration (CI)

Integrating testing into your development workflow through continuous integration (CI) systems can help catch issues early and ensure that your codebase remains stable. CI systems automatically build and test your game whenever changes are pushed to a version control repository.

Popular CI services like Travis CI, Jenkins, and GitHub Actions can be configured to run your unit tests, integration tests, and other automated checks automatically.

In conclusion, testing is an essential part of game development that helps ensure the quality and reliability of your SFML game. By incorporating unit testing, integration testing, functional testing, UI testing, playtesting, performance testing, regression testing, and CI into your development process, you can deliver a game that meets player expectations and provides a seamless gaming experience.

7.5 Handling Common Debugging Challenges

Debugging is an essential part of game development, but it can be challenging and time-consuming. In this section, we'll explore some common debugging challenges that you may encounter while developing your SFML game and provide strategies to overcome them.

1. Crashes and Segmentation Faults

One of the most frustrating issues is when your game crashes or encounters segmentation faults (segfaults). These issues often occur due to memory-related problems, such as dereferencing null or invalid pointers.

Strategy: Use Debugging Tools
- Utilize debugging tools like GDB (GNU Debugger) to pinpoint the exact location of the crash and examine the call stack.
- Analyze your code carefully, looking for potential null pointer dereferences or out-of-bounds array access.
- Enable compiler warnings and address any warnings or errors reported during compilation.

2. Memory Leaks

Memory leaks can lead to a gradual increase in memory usage, eventually causing your game to slow down or crash. Detecting memory leaks can be challenging, especially in complex games.

Strategy: Employ Memory Profilers

- Use memory profiling tools like Valgrind to identify memory leaks. Valgrind can provide detailed reports, including the exact location in your code where memory was allocated.
- Be diligent about releasing resources when they are no longer needed, especially in cases involving dynamically allocated memory (e.g., with `new` or `malloc`).

3. Performance Bottlenecks

Performance issues, such as low frame rates or high CPU usage, can negatively impact the player's experience. Identifying and addressing performance bottlenecks can be tricky.

Strategy: Profiling and Optimization

- Profile your game using built-in or external profilers to identify bottlenecks in your code.
- Optimize critical sections of your code, focusing on algorithmic improvements and reducing unnecessary calculations.
- Use data structures and algorithms that are better suited to your specific use case to improve performance.

4. Intermittent Bugs

Intermittent bugs, also known as "heisenbugs," are bugs that seem to appear and disappear unpredictably, making them challenging to reproduce and fix.

Strategy: Logging and Reproduction

- Implement extensive logging in your game to capture information about the game's state and events leading up to the bug.
- Encourage players and testers to report any bugs they encounter, even if they seem intermittent.
- Try to isolate the conditions that trigger the bug and create a reliable test case that reproduces it.

5. Platform-Specific Issues

SFML is designed to be cross-platform, but subtle platform-specific differences or bugs can still occur, especially when targeting multiple operating systems.

Strategy: Testing on Target Platforms

- Test your game on all target platforms to identify and address platform-specific issues.

- Keep up-to-date with SFML updates and community discussions to learn about platform-specific workarounds or solutions.

6. Multithreading Issues

Multithreading can introduce complex bugs related to race conditions, deadlocks, and data synchronization. Debugging multithreaded code can be challenging due to its non-deterministic nature.

Strategy: Thread-Safe Design and Debugging Tools
- Design your multithreaded code with thread safety in mind, using synchronization primitives like mutexes and condition variables.
- Use debugging tools like thread sanitizers and race detectors to identify and diagnose multithreading issues.

7. Networking and Online Play Issues

If your game includes networking and online features, debugging issues related to connectivity, server-client interactions, and synchronization can be complex.

Strategy: Logging and Network Monitoring
- Implement detailed network logging to trace network interactions and identify issues in communication.
- Use network monitoring tools to analyze the data being sent and received between clients and servers.
- Simulate different network conditions, such as latency and packet loss, to test your game's resilience to adverse network conditions.

8. Version Compatibility

As your game evolves and receives updates, ensuring compatibility with older versions can be a challenge, especially if you have a live player base.

Strategy: Versioning and Compatibility Testing
- Implement versioning mechanisms to ensure that clients and servers can communicate with compatible versions.
- Plan for backward compatibility when making changes to network protocols or data structures.
- Conduct compatibility testing with different versions of your game to catch compatibility issues early.

9. Game Logic Bugs

Bugs related to game logic, such as incorrect behavior or win/lose conditions, can be challenging to identify and reproduce.

Strategy: Unit Testing and Playtesting
- Write comprehensive unit tests for critical game logic components to catch logic bugs early.
- Conduct extensive playtesting to uncover gameplay-related issues, and gather feedback from players to refine game mechanics and rules.

In conclusion, debugging is an integral part of game development, and understanding how to address common challenges is crucial. Using a combination of debugging tools, profiling, testing, and systematic approaches, you can efficiently identify and resolve issues in your SFML game, ensuring a smoother and more enjoyable player experience.

Chapter 8: Extending Your Pong Game

8.1 Adding Sound and Music

Sound and music are essential components of game development that enhance the player's immersion and overall gaming experience. In this section, we'll explore how to incorporate sound effects and background music into your Pong game using the Simple and Fast Multimedia Library (SFML).

Understanding the Role of Sound in Games

Sound in games serves various purposes, including feedback, immersion, and storytelling. Sound effects can convey crucial information to players, such as confirming actions, indicating success or failure, or alerting them to in-game events. Music sets the tone, mood, and atmosphere of your game, enhancing the player's emotional engagement.

SFML's Audio Module

SFML provides a straightforward audio module that makes it easy to work with sounds and music in your game. This module allows you to:

- Load and play sound effects in various formats, such as WAV, MP3, and OGG.
- Stream and control background music for seamless transitions and looping.
- Adjust volume, pitch, and other audio properties to create dynamic audio experiences.

Adding Sound Effects

To add sound effects to your Pong game, follow these steps:

1. **Prepare Sound Files**: First, obtain or create the sound effect files you want to use in your game. Ensure they are in a compatible audio format (e.g., WAV, MP3).

2. **Load Sound Effects**: In your game code, load the sound effects using the `sf::SoundBuffer` class. For example:

```
sf::SoundBuffer ballHitBuffer;
if (!ballHitBuffer.loadFromFile("ball_hit.wav")) {
    // Handle error loading the sound file
}

// Create a sound object
sf::Sound ballHitSound;
ballHitSound.setBuffer(ballHitBuffer);
```

3. **Play Sound Effects**: Trigger sound effects in response to in-game events. For instance, play a sound effect when the ball hits a paddle:

```
if (ball.intersects(paddle)) {
    ballHitSound.play();
    // Handle collision logic
}
```

4. **Adjust Sound Properties**: You can adjust properties like volume, pitch, and position for a more dynamic audio experience. For example, to make a sound fade out:

```
ballHitSound.setVolume(50); // Set volume to 50%
ballHitSound.setPitch(1.2); // Increase pitch by 20%
```

Incorporating Background Music

To include background music in your Pong game, follow these steps:

1. **Prepare Music Files**: Obtain or create the music tracks you want to use in your game. Ensure they are in a compatible audio format (e.g., OGG, MP3).

2. **Load Background Music**: In your game code, load the background music using the `sf::Music` class:

```
sf::Music backgroundMusic;
if (!backgroundMusic.openFromFile("background_music.ogg")) {
    // Handle error loading the music file
}
```

3. **Play and Control Music**: Start playing the background music when your game starts. You can control playback, volume, and looping as needed:

```
backgroundMusic.play();
backgroundMusic.setVolume(50); // Set volume to 50%
backgroundMusic.setLoop(true); // Loop the music
```

Resource Management

Proper resource management is crucial when working with audio assets in your game. Make sure to load and release resources efficiently to prevent memory leaks and ensure optimal performance.

In conclusion, incorporating sound effects and music can elevate the overall gaming experience of your Pong game. SFML provides a straightforward audio module that simplifies the process of adding sound and music to your game, allowing you to create immersive and engaging auditory experiences for players.

8.2 Customizing Graphics and Themes

Customizing the graphics and themes of your Pong game can greatly enhance its visual appeal and make it stand out. In this section, we'll explore how to create custom graphics, design themes, and apply them to your Pong game using SFML.

Creating Custom Graphics

Custom graphics play a significant role in defining the look and feel of your game. You can design unique game elements such as paddles, balls, backgrounds, and user interfaces to match your game's theme. Here's how you can create custom graphics:

1. **Graphic Design Tools**: Use graphic design software like Adobe Photoshop, GIMP, or even simpler tools like Inkscape to create your game graphics. Ensure they have transparent backgrounds for seamless integration into your game.

2. **Choosing File Formats**: Save your graphics in appropriate formats, such as PNG or BMP, to maintain image quality while minimizing file size.

3. **Loading Graphics**: In your game code, use the `sf::Texture` class to load your custom graphics. For example:

```
sf::Texture paddleTexture;
if (!paddleTexture.loadFromFile("custom_paddle.png")) {
    // Handle error loading the texture
}
```

4. **Applying Graphics**: Apply your custom textures to game objects like paddles and balls by creating `sf::Sprite` objects:

```
sf::Sprite paddle;
paddle.setTexture(paddleTexture);
```

Designing Game Themes

A consistent and appealing visual theme can tie your game together and create a memorable player experience. When designing a theme, consider the following:

1. **Color Palette**: Choose a color palette that matches your game's mood and style. Consistency in color usage can make your game feel cohesive.

2. **Art Style**: Decide on an art style that suits your game, whether it's pixel art, cartoon, realistic, or something entirely unique. Stick to the chosen style throughout your game's graphics.

3. **UI Design**: Design user interface elements such as buttons, menus, and score displays to match your theme. Use appropriate fonts and styling to maintain consistency.

4. **Backgrounds**: Create background images or animations that complement your theme. Backgrounds can add depth and atmosphere to your game.

5. **Animations**: Consider adding animations to game elements to make them more engaging. Animations can include character movements, transitions, or particle effects.

Applying Themes to Your Game

Once you've designed custom graphics and established a theme, it's time to apply them to your Pong game:

1. **Replace Default Assets**: Replace default assets like paddles, balls, and backgrounds with your custom graphics. Update the code accordingly to use the new textures and sprites.

2. **Modify User Interface**: Customize the user interface elements, such as buttons and score displays, to reflect your chosen theme. Adjust fonts, colors, and layouts as needed.

3. **Consistency**: Ensure visual consistency across all game elements. The graphics, animations, and UI should all align with your theme.

4. **Testing and Feedback**: Playtest your game to see how the customized graphics and theme affect the player experience. Gather feedback from testers to make improvements.

5. **Optimization**: Keep an eye on performance. Custom graphics and animations can be resource-intensive, so optimize them to ensure smooth gameplay.

Dynamic Themes

Consider implementing dynamic themes that can change based on in-game events or player preferences. For example, you can have different themes for day and night or allow players to select their preferred theme from options. Dynamic themes can add variety and replay value to your game.

In conclusion, customizing graphics and themes can elevate the visual appeal of your Pong game and make it more engaging for players. Whether you're creating custom graphics, designing themes, or applying them to your game, thoughtful and consistent visual design can leave a lasting impression on your players and enhance their overall gaming experience.

8.3 Implementing Multiplayer Support

Adding multiplayer support to your Pong game can transform it into a dynamic and competitive experience that players can enjoy together. In this section, we'll explore how to implement multiplayer functionality using the Simple and Fast Multimedia Library (SFML).

Multiplayer Modes

Before diving into the implementation details, consider the multiplayer modes you want to offer in your Pong game. Here are a few common multiplayer modes for Pong:

1. **Local Multiplayer**: Players share a single device, with each controlling a paddle. This mode is suitable for couch gaming with friends.

2. **Online Multiplayer**: Players can connect over the internet to play against each other. This mode requires a server for handling game sessions.

3. **Split-Screen**: Players share a single device, but the screen is split to provide each player with a dedicated view. This mode is common in console games.

4. **LAN Multiplayer**: Players on the same local network can connect and play together. This mode is suitable for LAN parties or gatherings.

Local Multiplayer Implementation

Implementing local multiplayer in your Pong game involves creating and managing multiple player-controlled paddles. Here's a simplified outline of the process:

1. **Player Initialization**: Create instances of player-controlled paddles. You can assign different keys or controllers to each player for input.

2. **Input Handling**: Implement input handling logic to move each player's paddle based on their assigned controls. For example, player 1 might use the arrow keys, while player 2 uses the 'W' and 'S' keys.

3. **Collision Detection**: Ensure that the ball can collide with both paddles. Detect collisions with each paddle separately and update the ball's trajectory accordingly.

4. **Scoring**: Keep track of each player's score independently. Increase a player's score when the ball passes the opponent's paddle and enters the goal.

5. **Game Logic**: Implement win conditions and game-ending scenarios. Declare a winner when one player reaches a specified score or after a set number of rounds.

6. **User Interface**: Update the user interface to display both players' scores and relevant information, such as which player won a round.

Adding online multiplayer support to your Pong game is a more complex task and typically requires a server-client architecture. Here's an overview of the steps involved:

1. **Server Setup**: Set up a server to handle multiplayer game sessions. The server should manage player connections, game state synchronization, and matchmaking.

2. **Client-Server Communication**: Implement communication between clients and the server using networking protocols (e.g., TCP or UDP). Clients send and receive game state updates.

3. **Game State Synchronization**: Ensure that the game state is synchronized between all connected clients. This includes ball position, paddle positions, scores, and game events.

4. **Matchmaking**: Implement a matchmaking system that allows players to find opponents. This can involve creating game lobbies or rooms.

5. **Security**: Implement security measures to prevent cheating and ensure fair gameplay. This may include server-side validation of player actions.

6. **Disconnect Handling**: Handle disconnections gracefully. When a player disconnects, the game should continue for remaining players or resolve as needed.

7. **Scalability**: Ensure that the server can handle multiple game sessions simultaneously. Consider load balancing and server scaling as your player base grows.

8. **Testing and Optimization**: Thoroughly test the online multiplayer functionality and optimize network communication for minimal latency.

Split-Screen and LAN Multiplayer

Implementing split-screen or LAN multiplayer involves a combination of the techniques used in local and online multiplayer. Players share a single device or local network connection, and the game logic is similar to local multiplayer. However, you may need to adapt the user interface and input handling for split-screen play.

In conclusion, implementing multiplayer support in your Pong game can add a new dimension of excitement and competition. Whether you choose local, online, split-screen, or LAN multiplayer, careful planning and implementation are essential for creating a seamless and enjoyable multiplayer experience for your players.

8.4 Creating AI Opponents

Incorporating AI (Artificial Intelligence) opponents into your Pong game can provide a challenging and engaging single-player experience or complement your multiplayer mode.

In this section, we'll explore how to create AI opponents that can intelligently play Pong against the player.

To create effective AI opponents, you need to define their behavior and decision-making process. Here are some key considerations:

1. **Paddle Movement**: Decide how the AI-controlled paddle should move to intercept the ball. The AI should aim to position its paddle in a way that maximizes the chances of returning the ball.

2. **Difficulty Levels**: Implement multiple difficulty levels to cater to players with varying skill levels. Higher difficulty levels may involve faster and more accurate AI opponents.

3. **Predictive AI**: Advanced AI opponents can predict the ball's trajectory and adjust their paddle position accordingly. This adds a layer of challenge and realism.

4. **Reactive AI**: Simpler AI opponents can react to the ball's position and move their paddle in response. They may not predict the ball's path but can still offer a fun gaming experience.

Basic Reactive AI Implementation

Let's start by implementing a basic reactive AI opponent for your Pong game. Here's a simplified outline of the process:

1. **AI Initialization**: Create an AI-controlled paddle and set its initial position on the opposite side of the player's paddle.

2. **AI Movement Logic**: In the game loop, update the AI's paddle position based on the ball's current position. Calculate the vertical distance between the ball and the AI's paddle.

3. **Paddle Movement**: Move the AI's paddle up or down to align with the ball's position. You can adjust the AI's paddle speed to control how quickly it reacts.

4. **Limit Paddle Movement**: Ensure that the AI's paddle cannot move outside the game screen boundaries. Limit its movement to stay within the playable area.

5. **Difficulty Levels**: Implement multiple difficulty levels by adjusting the AI's reaction speed or accuracy. For example, a higher difficulty level may make the AI react faster to the ball's movement.

Here's a simplified code snippet in C++ to demonstrate the basic AI movement logic:

```
// Inside the game loop
sf::Vector2f ballPosition = ball.getPosition();
sf::Vector2f aiPaddlePosition = aiPaddle.getPosition();
```

```
// Calculate vertical distance between the ball and AI's paddle
float verticalDistance = ballPosition.y - aiPaddlePosition.y;

// Adjust the AI's paddle position based on the ball's position
if (verticalDistance > 0) {
    // Ball is below the AI's paddle, move it down
    aiPaddle.move(0, aiPaddleSpeed * deltaTime);
} else if (verticalDistance < 0) {
    // Ball is above the AI's paddle, move it up
    aiPaddle.move(0, -aiPaddleSpeed * deltaTime);
}
```

This basic AI logic makes the AI-controlled paddle react to the ball's position, attempting to intercept it. However, it doesn't predict the ball's trajectory, making it suitable for lower difficulty levels. For higher difficulty levels, you can implement more advanced predictive AI behavior.

In conclusion, adding AI opponents to your Pong game can enhance the single-player experience and provide a challenging opponent in multiplayer modes. Start with basic reactive AI, and if you want to increase the challenge, explore predictive AI techniques to create more formidable opponents for your players to face.

8.5 Enhancing User Experience

Enhancing the user experience (UX) in your Pong game is crucial to keep players engaged and satisfied. In this section, we'll explore various techniques and strategies to improve the overall user experience of your game.

Visual and Audio Feedback

1. **Responsive Controls**: Ensure that player inputs result in immediate and expected responses. Delayed or unresponsive controls can frustrate players.

2. **Visual Feedback**: Provide visual cues for important game events. For example, flash the ball when it hits the paddle, change the paddle's color when it scores a point, or display an explosion animation when a player wins.

3. **Audio Feedback**: Use sound effects and background music to enhance the game's atmosphere. Match sound effects to in-game actions, such as the sound of the ball hitting the paddle or the cheering of a crowd when a point is scored.

User Interface (UI) Design

1. **Clean and Intuitive UI**: Design a user interface that is easy to understand and navigate. Use clear labels and intuitive button placements for menus and options.

2. **Score Display**: Ensure that player scores are prominently displayed and easy to read. Consider using large, bold fonts and contrasting colors.

3. **Pause and Resume**: Implement a pause menu that allows players to pause the game, adjust settings, and resume play. Provide options for restarting or quitting the game.

Difficulty Levels

1. **Adjustable Difficulty**: Offer multiple difficulty levels to cater to players of different skill levels. Beginners may appreciate an easier mode, while experienced players may seek a challenge.

2. **Dynamic Difficulty**: Consider implementing a dynamic difficulty system that adapts to the player's performance. If a player consistently wins, increase the AI's skill level, and vice versa.

Game Progression

1. **Achievements and Rewards**: Implement achievements or milestones that players can strive to achieve. Reward players with in-game items, customization options, or simply recognition for their accomplishments.

2. **Unlockable Content**: Include unlockable content, such as new paddles, ball designs, or background themes. This gives players an incentive to continue playing and exploring the game.

Social and Multiplayer Features

1. **Leaderboards**: Implement online leaderboards that allow players to compete for high scores with others. Display the top players and their achievements.

2. **Multiplayer Modes**: If your game supports multiplayer, ensure that the matchmaking process is smooth, and players can easily find opponents. Provide options for both casual and competitive play.

Accessibility

1. **Customizable Controls**: Allow players to customize control inputs to accommodate their preferences and needs. Some players may require alternative control schemes.

2. **Subtitles and Language Support**: If your game includes dialogue or text, provide subtitles and support for multiple languages to make it accessible to a broader audience.

Testing and User Feedback

1. **Playtesting**: Regularly playtest your game with a diverse group of players. Gather feedback on their experiences and use it to identify areas for improvement.

2. **User Surveys**: Consider conducting surveys or collecting feedback from players to gauge their satisfaction and gather suggestions for enhancements.

Remember that the user experience is an ongoing process. Continuously gather feedback, analyze player behavior, and make iterative improvements to create a more enjoyable and engaging Pong game. By prioritizing user satisfaction, you can build a loyal player base and ensure the long-term success of your game.

Chapter 9: Building Tic-Tac-Toe

9.1 Designing the Tic-Tac-Toe Game

In this chapter, we'll delve into the development of Tic-Tac-Toe, a classic and simple two-player game. Before we start coding, it's essential to design the game to ensure a clear understanding of its components and rules.

Game Rules

Tic-Tac-Toe, also known as Noughts and Crosses, is played on a 3x3 grid. Two players take turns marking a square with their symbol, either 'X' or 'O'. The goal is to be the first to form a horizontal, vertical, or diagonal line of three of your symbols.

Here are the fundamental rules:

1. **Grid**: The game board is a 3x3 grid, totaling nine squares.

2. **Players**: There are two players: 'X' and 'O'.

3. **Turns**: Players take turns to place their symbol on an empty square.

4. **Winning**: The game ends when one player forms a winning line (horizontal, vertical, or diagonal) or when all squares are filled without a winner, resulting in a draw.

Game Components

Now, let's outline the key components and features of our Tic-Tac-Toe game:

1. **Game Board**: Create a 3x3 grid where players can place their symbols. Each square should be clickable and able to display 'X' or 'O'.

2. **Player Input**: Implement a mechanism for players to take turns and input their moves. This can be done through mouse clicks or touch events.

3. **Win Detection**: Develop a function to check for a winning condition after each move. It should identify if a player has won or if the game has ended in a draw.

4. **Feedback**: Provide visual feedback when a player wins or when the game ends in a draw. Highlight the winning line and display a message.

5. **Restart**: Allow players to restart the game after a win, loss, or draw. Provide a button or option to reset the board.

Game Flow

Here's a simplified flow of how the game progresses:

1. The game starts with an empty grid.

2. Players 'X' and 'O' take turns to make their moves.

3. After each move, the game checks for a winning condition or a draw.

4. If a player wins, the game displays a victory message and highlights the winning line.

5. If the game ends in a draw, it displays a draw message.

6. Players can choose to restart the game to play again.

In the upcoming sections, we will implement these components and the game's logic step by step. By starting with a clear design, we ensure that the development process is well-structured, making it easier to build a functional and enjoyable Tic-Tac-Toe game.

9.2 Implementing the Game Board

In this section, we will dive into the implementation of the game board for our Tic-Tac-Toe game. The game board serves as the canvas where players make their moves by placing 'X' or 'O' symbols. We'll break down the key steps to create and manage the game board.

Representing the Game Board

To represent the Tic-Tac-Toe game board, we can use a data structure such as a 2D array or a list of lists in many programming languages. Each cell in the grid can be empty, contain 'X', or contain 'O'. Here's a simple example in Python:

```python
# Initialize an empty 3x3 game board
board = [[' ' for _ in range(3)] for _ in range(3)]
```

In this representation, ' ' indicates an empty cell. When a player makes a move, we update the corresponding cell with their symbol ('X' or 'O').

Displaying the Game Board

Displaying the game board is essential for players to see the current state of the game. You can use various methods, depending on your chosen programming environment. For a command-line game, you might print the board like this:

```python
def print_board(board):
    for row in board:
        print('|'.join(row))
        print('-' * 5)
```

This function prints the current state of the game board with separators between cells.

Handling Player Input

To allow players to make moves, you need a mechanism to handle their input. This typically involves capturing their choice of row and column for their move. In a graphical game, you'd use mouse clicks or touch events. For a command-line game, you can prompt players to enter their move:

```python
def get_player_move():
    while True:
        try:
            row = int(input("Enter the row (0, 1, or 2): "))
            col = int(input("Enter the column (0, 1, or 2): "))
            if 0 <= row <= 2 and 0 <= col <= 2:
                return row, col
            else:
                print("Invalid input. Row and column must be between 0 and 2.")
        except ValueError:
            print("Invalid input. Please enter integers.")
```

This function prompts the player to enter row and column values, validates the input, and returns the chosen coordinates.

Updating the Game Board

After receiving a player's move, you need to update the game board to reflect the change. You'll set the chosen cell to 'X' or 'O'. Here's a basic example:

```python
def make_move(board, row, col, player):
    if board[row][col] == ' ':
        board[row][col] = player
        return True   # Move was successful
    else:
        return False  # Cell is already occupied
```

This function checks if the chosen cell is empty and, if so, updates it with the player's symbol.

In the next sections, we will cover how to implement win detection and game logic to create a fully functional Tic-Tac-Toe game.

9.3 Handling User Input for Tic-Tac-Toe

Handling user input is a crucial aspect of any interactive game, including Tic-Tac-Toe. In this section, we'll explore how to manage player input, validate moves, and ensure a smooth gaming experience.

Capturing Player Input

To allow players to make their moves in a Tic-Tac-Toe game, we need a method to capture their input. This can be achieved using various input methods depending on the platform you're developing for:

1. Graphical User Interface (GUI):

In a graphical game, you can implement mouse click or touch event handlers. When a player clicks or touches a cell on the game board, the corresponding row and column are determined from the click coordinates.

```
# Example pseudo-code for handling mouse click in a graphical game:
if mouse_clicked:
    row, col = determine_clicked_cell(mouse_x, mouse_y)
    if cell_is_empty(board, row, col):
        make_move(board, row, col, current_player)
```

2. Command-Line Interface (CLI):

For a command-line Tic-Tac-Toe game, you can prompt players to enter their move by specifying the row and column. Here's an example of how you might capture player input:

```
def get_player_move():
    while True:
        try:
            row = int(input("Enter the row (0, 1, or 2): "))
            col = int(input("Enter the column (0, 1, or 2): "))
            if 0 <= row <= 2 and 0 <= col <= 2:
                return row, col
            else:
                print("Invalid input. Row and column must be between 0 and 2.
")
        except ValueError:
            print("Invalid input. Please enter integers.")
```

Validating Player Moves

It's essential to validate player moves to ensure they are within the bounds of the game board and the selected cell is empty. This prevents invalid moves and cheating.

Here's how you can validate a player's move in a function:

```
def is_valid_move(board, row, col):
    return 0 <= row <= 2 and 0 <= col <= 2 and board[row][col] == ' '
```

You can use this function to check if a player's chosen move is valid before updating the game board.

Alternating Players

Tic-Tac-Toe is a turn-based game, so it's essential to alternate between players after each move. You can achieve this by keeping track of the current player and switching it at the end of each turn.

```python
def switch_player(current_player):
    return 'X' if current_player == 'O' else 'O'
```

After a player makes a valid move, you can call `switch_player` to switch to the other player's turn.

Implementing Game Logic

With input capture, move validation, and player switching in place, you have the foundations for the game logic. The overall game loop would look something like this:

```python
# Initialize the game board
board = [[' ' for _ in range(3)] for _ in range(3)]

# Initialize the current player (start with 'X')
current_player = 'X'

while True:
    print_board(board)

    # Get a valid move from the current player
    row, col = get_player_move()
    if is_valid_move(board, row, col):
        make_move(board, row, col, current_player)

        # Check for a win or draw
        if check_winner(board, current_player):
            print(f"Player {current_player} wins!")
            break
        elif is_board_full(board):
            print("It's a draw!")
            break

        # Switch to the other player's turn
        current_player = switch_player(current_player)
    else:
        print("Invalid move. Try again.")
```

This loop continues until there's a winner or a draw, providing players with a smooth and interactive experience. In the next section, we'll explore how to implement win conditions for Tic-Tac-Toe.

9.4 Implementing Win Conditions

In a game of Tic-Tac-Toe, determining the winner is a critical part of the gameplay. To create a satisfying gaming experience, you must implement win conditions that correctly identify when a player has won. In this section, we'll explore how to implement these conditions.

Win Conditions for Tic-Tac-Toe

Tic-Tac-Toe is a relatively simple game with eight possible win conditions. A player can win by having three of their symbols (either 'X' or 'O') in a row, column, or diagonal. Let's define the eight possible win conditions:

1. **Three Rows**: A player wins if they have three of their symbols in a horizontal row (top, middle, or bottom).
2. **Three Columns**: A player wins if they have three of their symbols in a vertical column (left, center, or right).
3. **Two Diagonals**: A player wins if they have three of their symbols in either of the two diagonals (from top-left to bottom-right or from top-right to bottom-left).

To check these win conditions in your code, you can create a function that analyzes the current state of the game board and returns the winning player or 'None' if there's no winner yet.

Here's a sample Python function to check for a win condition in a Tic-Tac-Toe game:

```python
def check_winner(board, player):
    # Check rows
    for row in board:
        if all(cell == player for cell in row):
            return player

    # Check columns
    for col in range(3):
        if all(board[row][col] == player for row in range(3)):
            return player

    # Check diagonals
    if all(board[i][i] == player for i in range(3)) or all(board[i][2 - i] ==
player for i in range(3)):
        return player

    return None   # No winner yet
```

In this code, we first check the rows and columns using nested loops. If we find a row or column where all three cells belong to the same player, we return that player as the winner. Then, we check both diagonals using individual conditions. If any of these conditions are met, we return the winning player. If none of the win conditions are met, we return 'None' to indicate that there's no winner yet.

Integrating Win Condition Checking

To integrate the win condition checking into your game loop (as demonstrated in the previous section), you can call the check_winner function after a player makes a move. If it returns a player, you can declare that player as the winner and end the game.

Here's how you can integrate win condition checking into the game loop:

```python
while True:
    print_board(board)

    # Get a valid move from the current player
    row, col = get_player_move()
    if is_valid_move(board, row, col):
        make_move(board, row, col, current_player)

        # Check for a win
        winner = check_winner(board, current_player)
        if winner:
            print(f"Player {winner} wins!")
            break

        # Check for a draw
        elif is_board_full(board):
            print("It's a draw!")
            break

        # Switch to the other player's turn
        current_player = switch_player(current_player)
    else:
        print("Invalid move. Try again.")
```

By implementing win conditions, you create a clear and satisfying outcome for your Tic-Tac-Toe game, making it more enjoyable for players.

9.5 Adding AI Opponent for Single-Player Mode

To enhance the single-player experience in your Tic-Tac-Toe game, you can add an AI opponent. This AI opponent will provide a challenging opponent for the player to compete against. In this section, we'll explore how to create a simple AI for Tic-Tac-Toe.

Creating a Simple AI

Creating a full-fledged AI for Tic-Tac-Toe can be quite complex, but we'll start with a basic implementation using a strategy called the "minimax" algorithm. The minimax algorithm is a decision-making algorithm used in two-player games to minimize the possible loss for a player. In Tic-Tac-Toe, the AI will try to find the best move that maximizes its chances of winning while minimizing the opponent's chances.

Here's a simplified implementation of a Tic-Tac-Toe AI using the minimax algorithm in Python:

```python
def minimax(board, depth, is_maximizing):
    if check_winner(board, 'X'):
        return -1
    if check_winner(board, 'O'):
        return 1
    if is_board_full(board):
        return 0

    if is_maximizing:
        best_score = -float('inf')
        for row in range(3):
            for col in range(3):
                if board[row][col] == '-':
                    board[row][col] = 'O'
                    score = minimax(board, depth + 1, False)
                    board[row][col] = '-'
                    best_score = max(score, best_score)
        return best_score
    else:
        best_score = float('inf')
        for row in range(3):
            for col in range(3):
                if board[row][col] == '-':
                    board[row][col] = 'X'
                    score = minimax(board, depth + 1, True)
                    board[row][col] = '-'
                    best_score = min(score, best_score)
        return best_score

def find_best_move(board):
    best_move = None
    best_score = -float('inf')
    for row in range(3):
        for col in range(3):
            if board[row][col] == '-':
                board[row][col] = 'O'
                score = minimax(board, 0, False)
                board[row][col] = '-'
                if score > best_score:
                    best_score = score
                    best_move = (row, col)
    return best_move
```

In this code, the `minimax` function recursively evaluates the game state for all possible moves and returns a score based on the current state. The AI aims to maximize its score while minimizing the player's score. The `find_best_move` function uses the minimax algorithm to find the best move for the AI based on the current board state.

Integrating the AI into the Game

To add the AI opponent to your Tic-Tac-Toe game, you can modify your game loop as follows:

```python
# Inside the game loop
if current_player == 'X':
    row, col = get_player_move()
    if is_valid_move(board, row, col):
        make_move(board, row, col, 'X')
    else:
        print("Invalid move. Try again.")
else:
    # AI's turn
    print("AI's turn:")
    row, col = find_best_move(board)
    make_move(board, row, col, 'O')
```

Now, when the AI's turn comes, it will use the minimax algorithm to make its move, providing a challenging opponent for the player in single-player mode.

10.1 Working with Text and Fonts

In game development, displaying text is a fundamental aspect of creating user interfaces, displaying scores, and conveying information to players. In this section, we will explore how to work with text and fonts in SFML to create dynamic and visually appealing text elements for your games.

Loading Fonts

Before you can display text in your game, you need to load a font. SFML supports various font file formats, such as TrueType (.ttf) and OpenType (.otf). You can find free fonts online or use your custom fonts to match your game's style.

Here's how you can load a font in SFML:

```cpp
sf::Font font;
if (!font.loadFromFile("arial.ttf")) {
    // Handle font loading error
}
```

In this example, we load the "arial.ttf" font. Make sure to provide the correct file path.

Creating Text Objects

Once you have loaded a font, you can create text objects. Text objects in SFML are instances of the `sf::Text` class. Here's how to create a basic text object:

```
sf::Text text;
text.setFont(font); // Set the font
text.setString("Hello, SFML!"); // Set the text content
text.setCharacterSize(24); // Set the character size
text.setFillColor(sf::Color::White); // Set the fill color
```

In this code, we set the font, text content, character size, and fill color for the text object. You can customize these properties to achieve the desired appearance for your text.

Positioning and Drawing Text

To display text on the screen, you need to specify its position and draw it within your game loop. Here's an example of how to do this:

```
text.setPosition(sf::Vector2f(100, 100)); // Set the position
// ...
while (window.isOpen()) {
    // ...
    window.clear();
    window.draw(text); // Draw the text
    window.display();
}
```

In this snippet, we set the position of the text using `setPosition` and then draw the text within the game loop using `window.draw(text)`.

Styling Text

SFML provides options to style your text, such as making it bold, italic, or underlined:

```
text.setStyle(sf::Text::Bold | sf::Text::Italic | sf::Text::Underlined);
```

You can combine these styles as needed to achieve the desired text appearance.

Text Alignment

You can control text alignment within its bounding box using the `setOrigin` and `setPosition` methods. These methods allow you to align text both horizontally and vertically:

```
// Center the text horizontally and vertically within its bounding box
text.setOrigin(text.getLocalBounds().width / 2, text.getLocalBounds().height
/ 2);
text.setPosition(sf::Vector2f(window.getSize().x / 2, window.getSize().y / 2)
);
```

In this code, we center the text both horizontally and vertically within the window.

Wrapping Text

If your text exceeds a certain width, you may want to wrap it to the next line. SFML doesn't provide automatic text wrapping, but you can implement a custom solution by measuring the text's width and breaking it into lines accordingly.

Conclusion

Working with text and fonts in SFML allows you to create informative and visually appealing user interfaces for your games. By loading fonts, creating text objects, styling text, and controlling alignment, you can display text effectively within your game's environment. Experiment with different fonts, sizes, and styles to achieve the desired look and feel for your game's text elements.

10.2 Utilizing Sprites and Textures

In game development, graphics play a crucial role in creating immersive and engaging experiences. SFML provides a straightforward way to work with graphics, including sprites and textures. In this section, we'll explore how to utilize sprites and textures to display images and graphics in your games.

Loading Textures

Before you can use sprites to display images, you need to load textures. Textures represent image data in SFML and serve as the source material for sprites. Here's how you can load a texture:

```
sf::Texture texture;
if (!texture.loadFromFile("image.png")) {
    // Handle texture loading error
}
```

In this example, we load the "image.png" texture. Ensure that you provide the correct file path to the image.

Creating Sprites

Sprites in SFML are instances of the sf::Sprite class. To create a sprite and associate it with a texture, you can do the following:

```
sf::Sprite sprite;
sprite.setTexture(texture); // Set the texture
```

Now, the sprite object is associated with the loaded texture. You can position, scale, and manipulate the sprite as needed to display it within your game.

Positioning and Drawing Sprites

To display a sprite on the screen, you need to set its position and draw it within your game loop:

```
sprite.setPosition(sf::Vector2f(100, 100)); // Set the position
// ...
while (window.isOpen()) {
    // ...
    window.clear();
    window.draw(sprite); // Draw the sprite
    window.display();
}
```

In this code, we set the position of the sprite using setPosition and then draw the sprite within the game loop using window.draw(sprite).

Scaling and Rotating Sprites

SFML allows you to scale and rotate sprites to achieve various visual effects. For example, you can scale a sprite by a factor of 2:

```
sprite.setScale(sf::Vector2f(2, 2)); // Scale the sprite by a factor of 2
```

You can also rotate a sprite by a specified angle in degrees:

```
sprite.setRotation(45); // Rotate the sprite by 45 degrees
```

These transformations can be useful for animations, zooming effects, and other visual enhancements in your game.

Sprite Origin

The origin of a sprite defines the point around which transformations like rotation and scaling occur. By default, the origin is set to the top-left corner of the sprite. You can change the origin using the setOrigin method:

```
sprite.setOrigin(sf::Vector2f(sprite.getLocalBounds().width / 2, sprite.getLo
calBounds().height / 2));
```

In this code, we set the origin to the center of the sprite, making it easier to rotate and scale around the center.

Conclusion

Utilizing sprites and textures in SFML allows you to incorporate images and graphics into your games. By loading textures, creating sprites, positioning them, and applying transformations, you can display visual elements that enhance the gameplay and user experience. Experiment with different textures, positions, scales, and rotations to achieve the desired visual effects in your games.

10.3 Managing Animation

Animation adds life and excitement to games. It allows you to create dynamic and visually appealing experiences for players. In this section, we'll explore how to manage animations in SFML.

Frame-Based Animation

One common approach to animation is frame-based animation. It involves displaying a sequence of images (frames) in rapid succession to create the illusion of motion. Each frame represents a different state of the object being animated.

To implement frame-based animation in SFML, you typically follow these steps:

1. Load multiple textures, each representing a frame of the animation.

2. Create a sprite to display the current frame.

3. Update the sprite's texture to switch between frames at a certain frame rate.

4. Draw the sprite on the screen.

Here's a simplified example:

```
sf::Texture frame1, frame2, frame3;
frame1.loadFromFile("frame1.png");
frame2.loadFromFile("frame2.png");
frame3.loadFromFile("frame3.png");

sf::Sprite sprite;
sprite.setTexture(frame1);

sf::Clock clock;
float frameRate = 0.1f; // Time (in seconds) between frame changes
float elapsedTime = 0.0f;

while (window.isOpen()) {
    float deltaTime = clock.restart().asSeconds();
    elapsedTime += deltaTime;

    if (elapsedTime >= frameRate) {
        // Switch to the next frame
        if (sprite.getTexture() == &frame1) {
            sprite.setTexture(frame2);
        } else if (sprite.getTexture() == &frame2) {
            sprite.setTexture(frame3);
        } else {
            sprite.setTexture(frame1);
```

```
    }
        elapsedTime = 0.0f;
    }

    window.clear();
    window.draw(sprite);
    window.display();
}
```

In this code, we load three frames as textures and switch between them using a clock to control the frame rate.

Using Sprite Sheets

For more complex animations, sprite sheets are a common choice. A sprite sheet is a single image that contains multiple frames arranged in a grid or sequence. You can use different parts of the image as individual frames.

SFML provides a `sf::IntRect` class to define the rectangular region of the sprite sheet to display as a frame. You can use it in combination with the `setTextureRect` method to select specific frames.

Conclusion

Animation is an essential aspect of game development that enhances player engagement and visual appeal. SFML provides the necessary tools to implement animations, whether through frame-based animation with multiple textures or sprite sheets. Experiment with different frame rates, frame sequences, and sprite sheet layouts to create captivating animations for your games.

10.4 Implementing Special Effects

Special effects can greatly enhance the visual appeal of your games and make them more immersive. SFML provides various ways to implement special effects, from basic techniques to more advanced ones. In this section, we'll explore some common special effects and how to implement them using SFML.

Particle Systems

Particle systems are a versatile and efficient way to create various visual effects, such as smoke, fire, rain, or explosions. SFML doesn't have a built-in particle system, but you can create one easily by managing a collection of particles (e.g., sprites) and updating their positions, sizes, and lifetimes over time.

Here's a simplified example of a basic particle system in SFML:

```
// Initialize particles with random positions, velocities, and lifetimes
std::vector<sf::CircleShape> particles;
```

```
for (int i = 0; i < 100; ++i) {
    sf::CircleShape particle(2.0f);
    particle.setFillColor(sf::Color::Yellow);
    particle.setPosition(sf::Vector2f(rand() % 800, rand() % 600));
    sf::Vector2f velocity(rand() % 200 - 100, rand() % 200 - 100);
    float lifetime = 1.0f + static_cast<float>(rand()) / RAND_MAX * 3.0f;

    particles.push_back(particle);
}

sf::Clock clock;

while (window.isOpen()) {
    float deltaTime = clock.restart().asSeconds();

    // Update particle positions based on their velocities
    for (sf::CircleShape& particle : particles) {
        sf::Vector2f velocity = /* update velocity based on forces */;
        particle.move(velocity * deltaTime);
    }

    window.clear();

    // Draw all particles
    for (const sf::CircleShape& particle : particles) {
        window.draw(particle);
    }

    window.display();
}
```

In this example, we create a simple particle system by spawning circles with random positions, velocities, and lifetimes. Over time, the particles move according to their velocities, creating the illusion of motion.

Shaders

Shaders are a powerful tool for creating various visual effects in SFML. They are small programs that run on the GPU and can manipulate the appearance of objects or the entire screen. You can use shaders to achieve effects like post-processing, distortion, blur, and more.

To use shaders in SFML, you need to create a sf::Shader object, load a shader file (usually in GLSL), and apply it to the render target (e.g., the window). Shaders allow you to manipulate the color, position, and other attributes of pixels in real-time.

```
sf::Shader shader;
shader.loadFromFile("shader.frag", sf::Shader::Fragment);
```

```
while (window.isOpen()) {
    // Apply the shader to the entire window
    window.draw(/* objects to render */);
    window.draw(/* more objects to render */);
    window.display();
}
```

In this code, we load a fragment shader from a file and apply it to the render target. The shader file can contain custom code to achieve various visual effects.

Screen Transitions

Screen transitions, like fading in or out between scenes, can add a polished feel to your games. You can implement screen transitions by overlaying a semi-transparent rectangle on the screen and gradually changing its opacity over time.

Here's a simplified example of fading in:

```
sf::RectangleShape fadeOverlay(sf::Vector2f(window.getSize().x, window.getSiz
e().y));
fadeOverlay.setFillColor(sf::Color(0, 0, 0, 255)); // Fully opaque black

sf::Clock clock;
float fadeDuration = 2.0f; // 2 seconds fade-in duration

while (window.isOpen()) {
    float deltaTime = clock.restart().asSeconds();
    float fadeSpeed = 255 / fadeDuration;

    // Decrease opacity
    int alpha = fadeOverlay.getFillColor().a - static_cast<int>(fadeSpeed * d
eltaTime);
    if (alpha < 0) alpha = 0;
    fadeOverlay.setFillColor(sf::Color(0, 0, 0, alpha));

    window.clear();
    window.draw(/* objects to render */);
    window.draw(fadeOverlay);
    window.display();
}
```

In this example, we create a semi-transparent black rectangle and decrease its opacity over time, creating a fade-in effect.

These are just a few examples of the special effects you can implement in SFML. Experiment with different techniques, combine them, and customize them to suit your game's style and atmosphere. Special effects can make your games more visually appealing and engaging.

10.5 Creating a User Interface (UI)

In game development, creating a user interface (UI) is crucial for providing players with information, options, and interactivity. A well-designed UI enhances the player's experience and makes the game more accessible. SFML doesn't have built-in UI components like some other libraries or engines, but you can create your own custom UI using SFML's rendering and input handling capabilities. In this section, we'll explore how to design and implement a basic game UI.

UI Elements

A game UI typically consists of various elements, such as buttons, text labels, input fields, and menus. You can use SFML's `sf::Text` and `sf::RectangleShape` for rendering text and simple shapes as UI elements. Here's an example of creating a basic button with SFML:

```cpp
sf::RectangleShape button(sf::Vector2f(200, 50)); // Button with width 200 an
d height 50
button.setFillColor(sf::Color::Green);

sf::Text buttonText("Click Me!", font, 24); // Text with "Click Me!" using a
specific font and size
buttonText.setFillColor(sf::Color::White);
buttonText.setPosition(100, 25); // Center text inside the button

while (window.isOpen()) {
    // Handle input, e.g., mouse clicks
    if (sf::Mouse::isButtonPressed(sf::Mouse::Left)) {
        sf::Vector2i mousePosition = sf::Mouse::getPosition(window);
        if (button.getGlobalBounds().contains(static_cast<sf::Vector2f>(mouse
Position))) {
            // Button clicked
            // Implement your button action here
        }
    }

    window.clear();
    window.draw(button);
    window.draw(buttonText);
    window.display();
}
```

In this code, we create a green rectangular button with white text inside it. We then check for mouse clicks and detect if the click happened within the button's boundaries, allowing us to trigger an action when the button is clicked.

Designing a clean and organized UI layout is essential for user-friendliness. You can use SFML's positioning and alignment to arrange UI elements effectively. Here's an example of aligning UI elements within a menu:

```
sf::Text title("Main Menu", font, 36);
title.setFillColor(sf::Color::White);
title.setPosition(400 - title.getLocalBounds().width / 2, 50);

sf::RectangleShape startButton(sf::Vector2f(200, 50));
startButton.setFillColor(sf::Color::Green);
sf::Text startButtonText("Start Game", font, 24);
startButtonText.setFillColor(sf::Color::White);
startButtonText.setPosition(400 - startButtonText.getLocalBounds().width / 2,
150);

sf::RectangleShape exitButton(sf::Vector2f(200, 50));
exitButton.setFillColor(sf::Color::Red);
sf::Text exitButtonText("Exit", font, 24);
exitButtonText.setFillColor(sf::Color::White);
exitButtonText.setPosition(400 - exitButtonText.getLocalBounds().width / 2, 2
50);

while (window.isOpen()) {
    // Handle button clicks as shown in the previous example

    window.clear();
    window.draw(title);
    window.draw(startButton);
    window.draw(startButtonText);
    window.draw(exitButton);
    window.draw(exitButtonText);
    window.display();
}
```

In this code, we align the title and two buttons vertically within the menu, ensuring that they are centered on the screen. Proper alignment and spacing enhance the UI's visual appeal and usability.

User Feedback

Feedback is essential to inform players about game events and their progress. You can use SFML to display messages, notifications, and status indicators. Here's a simple example of displaying a message when a button is clicked:

```
bool buttonClicked = false;

while (window.isOpen()) {
    if (sf::Mouse::isButtonPressed(sf::Mouse::Left) && !buttonClicked) {
```

```
        sf::Vector2i mousePosition = sf::Mouse::getPosition(window);
        if (button.getGlobalBounds().contains(static_cast<sf::Vector2f>(mouse
Position))) {
            buttonClicked = true;
            // Display a message
            sf::Text message("Button Clicked!", font, 24);
            message.setFillColor(sf::Color::White);
            message.setPosition(400 - message.getLocalBounds().width / 2, 350
);

            window.clear();
            window.draw(button);
            window.draw(buttonText);
            window.draw(message);
            window.display();
        }
    }
    // ...
}
```

In this example, we add a boolean flag buttonClicked to ensure that the message is displayed only once when the button is clicked. This feedback informs the player that their action was successful.

Creating a game UI in SFML involves designing UI elements, arranging them in a layout, and providing user feedback. With these concepts, you can start implementing your custom game UI to enhance player interaction

Chapter 11: Building a Mario-Style Platformer

In this chapter, we will dive into the exciting world of platformer game development using SFML. Platformer games are a beloved genre known for their engaging gameplay and iconic characters. We'll explore the fundamental concepts and techniques required to create a Mario-style platformer from scratch.

Section 11.1: Designing the Platformer Game

Before we start coding, it's essential to plan our platformer game. In this section, we will discuss the design aspects, including character movement, level design, and game mechanics. Proper planning is key to creating a fun and challenging platformer experience.

Section 11.2: Creating Player Character and Controls

The heart of any platformer game is its player character. In this section, we'll create a player character sprite and implement controls for movement and jumping. We'll also explore techniques for smooth character animations.

Physics and collision detection are crucial for realistic and responsive gameplay. We'll delve into these topics, covering concepts like gravity, collision detection, and collision response. You'll learn how to handle collisions between the player character and the game world.

A well-designed level can make or break a platformer game. We'll discuss level design principles and techniques, including creating maps and integrating them into the game. We'll also look at tools and approaches for level design.

No platformer is complete without adversaries and challenges. We'll add enemy characters, obstacles, and various gameplay elements to make our platformer exciting and engaging. You'll learn how to design and implement these elements effectively.

Building a Mario-style platformer is a fantastic way to apply your SFML skills and create a game that's both enjoyable to play and a great learning experience. Let's embark on this journey to create a classic platformer game!

Chapter 11: Building a Mario-Style Platformer

Section 11.1: Designing the Platformer Game

Designing a Mario-style platformer game requires careful thought and planning. These games are known for their charming characters, challenging levels, and entertaining gameplay. In this section, we will explore the essential aspects of designing such a game.

Game Concept

The first step in designing any game is to come up with a compelling concept. For a platformer game, consider the following:

- **Theme:** Decide on the game's theme and setting. Will it be a classic 2D platformer with a side-scrolling perspective? What will be the main character's role or mission?

- **Characters:** Create a list of characters, including the protagonist (player character) and any enemies or allies. Each character should have distinct traits and abilities.

- **Levels:** Outline the game's structure, including the number of levels or worlds and their themes. Think about the progression of difficulty.

Player Mechanics

One of the defining features of platformer games is the player's control over the main character. Consider the following mechanics:

- **Movement:** Determine how the character will move. Common actions include running, jumping, and ducking. Decide if there are any special abilities.

- **Physics:** Define the game's physics, including gravity, friction, and how the character interacts with surfaces. These factors greatly impact gameplay.

- **Health and Lives:** Decide how the player's health and lives will work. Will there be power-ups or checkpoints?

Level Design

Creating engaging levels is critical to a platformer's success. Here are some level design considerations:

- **Obstacles:** Plan the types of obstacles and challenges players will encounter. These can include gaps, spikes, enemies, and moving platforms.

- **Collectibles:** Think about collectible items like coins or power-ups. How will they affect gameplay, and what rewards will they offer?

- **Progression:** Ensure a smooth progression of difficulty. Early levels should introduce mechanics gradually, while later levels should provide more significant challenges.

Visuals and Audio

The visual and audio aspects of your game contribute to its overall atmosphere and appeal:

- **Art Style:** Choose an art style that suits your game's theme and character designs. Ensure visual consistency throughout the game.

- **Soundtrack:** Consider the music and sound effects that will accompany the gameplay. Music can greatly enhance the player's experience.

Testing and Iteration

Throughout the design process, it's essential to playtest your game and gather feedback. Make adjustments based on user testing to improve gameplay, fix issues, and ensure that the game is fun and balanced.

Remember that designing a platformer game is a creative process, and there's no one-size-fits-all approach. Take inspiration from classic platformers but also bring your unique ideas to the table. With careful planning and attention to detail, you can create an enjoyable Mario-style platformer game that players will love.

Section 11.2: Creating Player Character and Controls

In a Mario-style platformer game, the player character is the heart of the experience. This section will focus on designing and implementing the player character and the controls that players will use to interact with the game world.

Designing the Player Character

Before you dive into coding, it's essential to design your player character thoroughly. Consider the following aspects:

Character Appearance and Personality

- **Visual Design:** Create a visually appealing character that fits the game's theme. The character's appearance should be distinct, making it easily recognizable.

- **Personality:** Think about the character's personality and how it reflects in their animations and interactions with the game world. Are they brave, goofy, or determined?

Abilities and Special Moves

- **Basic Abilities:** Define the character's basic abilities, such as running, jumping, and crouching. These form the foundation of the character's interactions.

- **Special Moves:** Consider if the character will have any special moves or abilities. For example, Mario can perform a high jump by pressing and holding the jump button for a longer time.

Physics and Movement

- **Physics:** Decide on the character's physics, including parameters like gravity, friction, and acceleration. These factors significantly impact how the character moves and interacts with the environment.

- **Controls:** Plan the control scheme for your character. Will you use keyboard inputs, gamepad controls, or touch screen gestures? Ensure that the controls are intuitive and responsive.

Implementing the Player Character

Once you've designed your player character, it's time to implement it in your game engine or framework. Here are some steps to get you started:

Character Sprites and Animations

- **Sprite Sheets:** Create or obtain sprite sheets for your character's animations. These sheets contain multiple frames of the character's animations, such as walking, jumping, and idle poses.

- **Animation System:** Implement an animation system that can cycle through the sprite frames to create smooth animations. Depending on your game engine, you may need to write code to manage this.

Collision Detection

- **Collision Shapes:** Define the collision shapes for your character. Usually, characters have a bounding box or a simple shape that represents their hitbox.

- **Collision Detection:** Implement collision detection logic to check if the character collides with other objects in the game world. This is crucial for handling interactions with platforms, obstacles, and enemies.

Movement and Controls

- **Movement Logic:** Write code to handle the character's movement based on user input. This includes code for walking, jumping, and other actions.

- **Physics Integration:** Apply the physics parameters you defined to govern how the character responds to gravity, ground friction, and other physical forces.

Feedback and Feedback

- **Visual Feedback:** Implement visual feedback for character actions, such as particle effects when jumping or landing.

- **Audio Feedback:** Add sound effects that correspond to the character's actions, like footsteps or jumping sounds.

Remember that creating a player character is an iterative process. You may need to fine-tune animations, adjust movement physics, and playtest extensively to ensure that controlling the character feels satisfying and fun. Additionally, consider adding features like character upgrades or power-ups to enhance gameplay and player engagement.

Section 11.3: Implementing Physics and Collision

In a Mario-style platformer game, accurate physics and collision detection are crucial for creating a believable and engaging game world. This section will guide you through implementing physics for your game character and handling collision interactions with the environment.

Physics for Player Character

To make your player character move and interact realistically with the game world, consider the following physics components:

1. Gravity

Implement a gravity system that pulls the character downward. Gravity gives the character weight and makes jumping and falling feel natural. You can define a constant gravitational force and apply it to the character's vertical velocity.

```
// Apply gravity to the character's velocity
characterVelocity.y += gravity * deltaTime;
```

2. Velocity and Acceleration

Track the character's velocity and acceleration to determine how they move. Apply acceleration when the player presses movement keys and update the character's position based on velocity.

```
// Apply acceleration based on player input (e.g., left or right)
if (isMovingLeft) {
    characterAcceleration.x = -moveSpeed;
} else if (isMovingRight) {
    characterAcceleration.x = moveSpeed;
} else {
    characterAcceleration.x = 0.0f;
}
```

```
// Update velocity based on acceleration
characterVelocity += characterAcceleration * deltaTime;
```

```
// Update character position based on velocity
characterPosition += characterVelocity * deltaTime;
```

3. Jumping

Implement a jumping mechanism that allows the character to jump off the ground. Ensure that the character can jump only when grounded, and adjust the vertical velocity accordingly.

```
if (isJumping && isGrounded) {
    // Apply an upward impulse for jumping
    characterVelocity.y = -jumpForce;
}
```

Collision Detection and Response

Accurate collision detection is vital to prevent the character from passing through solid objects and platforms. Consider these aspects:

1. Collision Shapes

Define collision shapes for both the character and the environment objects (e.g., platforms, walls). Common shapes include rectangles for simplicity.

```
sf::FloatRect characterBounds = character.getGlobalBounds();
sf::FloatRect platformBounds = platform.getGlobalBounds();
```

2. Collision Detection

Check for collisions between the character and environment objects. You can use bounding box intersection tests to detect collisions.

```
if (characterBounds.intersects(platformBounds)) {
    // Collision detected; handle it here
}
```

3. Collision Response

When a collision occurs, respond appropriately to prevent the character from overlapping with the object. Implement mechanisms like resolving the character's position or changing its velocity.

```
// Example of resolving position to avoid overlap
if (characterBounds.intersects(platformBounds)) {
    sf::Vector2f overlap = characterBounds.intersection(platformBounds);
    characterPosition -= overlap;
}
```

Optimizing Collision Detection

Efficient collision detection is essential, especially in complex game levels. Consider using data structures like spatial partitioning (e.g., quadtree) to optimize collision checks. These structures reduce the number of collision checks by narrowing down the potential colliding objects.

Additionally, fine-tuning collision detection and response is an iterative process. Test your character's interactions with various objects, platforms, and obstacles in your game world, and make adjustments as needed to ensure smooth and believable physics and collision interactions.

Section 11.4: Designing Levels and Maps

In a Mario-style platformer game, designing engaging levels and maps is a critical aspect of creating an enjoyable player experience. This section will explore the principles and techniques for designing levels, including layout, challenges, and progression.

1. Layout and Flow

A well-designed level should have a clear layout and flow that guides the player through the game world. Consider the following aspects:

- **Progression**: Levels should start with simpler challenges and gradually increase in difficulty. The player should feel a sense of accomplishment as they progress.

- **Exploration**: Encourage exploration by including hidden areas, collectibles, and secrets. These can provide rewards and add depth to the gameplay.

- **Landmarks**: Use landmarks and visual cues to help players orient themselves within the level. This can include distinctive background elements or recurring themes.

- **Pacing**: Control the pacing of the level by varying the intensity of challenges. Mix platforming segments with moments of calm exploration or storytelling.

2. Obstacles and Challenges

Challenges are at the heart of platformer gameplay. Create a variety of obstacles to keep players engaged:

- **Jumping Challenges**: Design platforms with different heights and distances to require precise jumps. Include moving platforms or platforms that disappear after a time.

- **Enemies**: Introduce enemies with unique behaviors and attack patterns. Consider how enemies fit into the level's theme and challenges.

- **Puzzles**: Incorporate puzzles that require logical thinking or coordination. Puzzles can add depth to the gameplay and offer a break from action segments.

- **Environmental Hazards**: Create hazards like spikes, bottomless pits, or falling objects. These hazards should be clearly telegraphed to give players a chance to react.

3. Theme and Aesthetics

A cohesive theme and aesthetics can enhance the player's immersion in the game world:

- **Visual Theme**: Choose a consistent visual theme for the level. This can be based on the game's overall art style and narrative.

- **Background Elements**: Add background elements that complement the level's theme. These elements can help convey the setting and atmosphere.

- **Music and Sound**: Use music and sound effects to enhance the mood and atmosphere of the level. Consider how music changes based on the player's progress or events in the level.

4. Playtesting and Iteration

Testing your levels thoroughly is essential. Playtest the level yourself and consider seeking feedback from others. Look for areas where players may get stuck or frustrated and make adjustments accordingly.

Iterate on your level designs to refine them. This may involve tweaking enemy placements, adjusting the timing of obstacles, or adding hints to guide players.

5. User-Friendly Design

Finally, aim for user-friendly level design. Ensure that your levels are accessible and enjoyable for players of varying skill levels. Include checkpoints or save points to prevent players from having to replay long sections after failures.

Remember that level design is both an art and a science. It requires creativity, but it also benefits from systematic testing and refinement. By applying these principles and techniques, you can create levels that provide a satisfying and memorable gameplay experience in your Mario-style platformer game.

Section 11.5: Adding Enemies and Challenges

Enemies and challenges are fundamental elements of a Mario-style platformer game, adding excitement and complexity to the gameplay. In this section, we'll explore how to design and implement enemies and various challenges to keep players engaged and entertained.

1. Types of Enemies

Enemies can take various forms, each with its own behavior and characteristics:

- **Ground Enemies**: These enemies move along the ground and typically follow a predictable path. Examples include Goombas and Koopa Troopas.

- **Flying Enemies**: Flying enemies add verticality to the game. They can move horizontally or follow more complex patterns. Examples include Paratroopas and Bullet Bills.

- **Stationary Enemies**: Some enemies remain in one place but may have deadly projectiles or other attacks. Piranha Plants are a classic example.

- **Bosses**: Boss battles are significant events in platformer games. Boss enemies are larger, more challenging, and often require unique strategies to defeat.

2. Enemy Behavior

To create engaging encounters, consider the following aspects of enemy behavior:

- **Movement Patterns**: Define how enemies move. This can include walking, jumping, flying, or even teleporting. Vary movement patterns to keep players on their toes.

- **Attack Patterns**: Determine how enemies attack the player. This might involve shooting projectiles, charging at the player, or using special abilities.

- **Vulnerabilities**: Enemies should have vulnerabilities or weaknesses that the player can exploit. For example, jumping on an enemy's head may defeat it.

- **Reactions**: Consider how enemies react to the player's actions. Some enemies may chase the player, while others may flee when approached.

3. Challenges and Obstacles

Challenges go beyond enemies and can include various obstacles that test the player's platforming skills:

- **Platforming Challenges**: Create platforms that require precise jumping or timing to traverse. Add moving platforms, conveyor belts, or collapsing platforms for variety.

- **Puzzles**: Incorporate puzzles that involve interacting with the environment to progress. This might include switches, levers, or pressure plates.

- **Collectibles**: Place collectible items throughout the level to encourage exploration and reward players for their efforts. Collectibles can be used to unlock secrets or power-ups.

- **Time-Based Challenges**: Some levels may include time-based challenges, such as escaping a collapsing area or racing against the clock.

4. Power-Ups

Power-ups are a classic element of Mario-style platformers and can significantly impact gameplay:

- **Super Mushrooms**: These make the player character larger and grant an extra hit point.

- **Fire Flowers**: Fire Flowers allow the player to shoot projectiles and defeat enemies from a distance.

- **Invincibility Stars**: Collecting an invincibility star grants temporary invulnerability and the ability to defeat enemies by touching them.

- **Other Power-Ups**: Depending on your game's design, you can introduce various other power-ups that enhance gameplay or provide unique abilities.

5. Balancing Difficulty

Balancing the difficulty of enemies and challenges is crucial to ensure that players find the game challenging but not frustrating. Playtesting is essential to fine-tune enemy placements, attack patterns, and obstacles.

Consider providing multiple difficulty levels or adjustable settings to accommodate a broader range of players, from beginners to experts.

In conclusion, adding enemies and challenges to your Mario-style platformer game can elevate the gameplay experience. Careful design and testing are essential to create engaging, balanced, and enjoyable levels that keep players coming back for more.

Chapter 12: Handling Input Devices

Section 12.1: Keyboard Input Handling

Keyboard input is a fundamental aspect of game development, allowing players to interact with your game and control characters or objects. In this section, we will explore how to handle keyboard input in your game using SFML.

1. Setting Up the Keyboard Input

To handle keyboard input in SFML, you need to include the appropriate header and create an SFML RenderWindow object. Here's a basic setup in C++:

```cpp
#include <SFML/Graphics.hpp>

int main() {
    sf::RenderWindow window(sf::VideoMode(800, 600), "SFML Keyboard Input");

    while (window.isOpen()) {
        sf::Event event;
        while (window.pollEvent(event)) {
            if (event.type == sf::Event::Closed) {
                window.close();
            }
        }

        // Handle keyboard input here

        window.clear();
        // Draw your game objects here
        window.display();
    }

    return 0;
}
```

2. Detecting Key Presses

SFML provides an easy way to check if a key is pressed. You can use the sf::Keyboard::isKeyPressed function to determine if a specific key is currently pressed. For example, to check if the "A" key is pressed:

```cpp
if (sf::Keyboard::isKeyPressed(sf::Keyboard::A)) {
    // The "A" key is currently pressed
}
```

3. Handling Continuous Input

Sometimes, you may need to handle continuous input, such as moving a character when a key is held down. You can achieve this by tracking the state of keys in each frame. Here's an example of moving an object when the arrow keys are held down:

```cpp
sf::Vector2f position(400.0f, 300.0f);
float speed = 5.0f;

while (window.isOpen()) {
    // ...

    if (sf::Keyboard::isKeyPressed(sf::Keyboard::Left)) {
        position.x -= speed;
    }
    if (sf::Keyboard::isKeyPressed(sf::Keyboard::Right)) {
        position.x += speed;
    }
    if (sf::Keyboard::isKeyPressed(sf::Keyboard::Up)) {
        position.y -= speed;
    }
    if (sf::Keyboard::isKeyPressed(sf::Keyboard::Down)) {
        position.y += speed;
    }

    // ...
}
```

4. Handling Key Releases

You can also detect when a key is released using the sf::Event system. For example, to detect when the "Space" key is released:

```cpp
while (window.pollEvent(event)) {
    if (event.type == sf::Event::Closed) {
        window.close();
    }
    else if (event.type == sf::Event::KeyReleased && event.key.code == sf::Keyboard::Space) {
        // The "Space" key was released
    }
}
```

5. Handling Text Input

If your game involves text input, you can use SFML's text input events to capture and display text entered by the player. This allows for creating features like naming characters or entering text-based commands.

In summary, handling keyboard input in your game is crucial for player interaction and control. SFML provides simple and effective methods to detect key presses, releases, and continuous input, allowing you to create responsive and engaging gameplay experiences.

Section 12.2: Mouse Input Handling

Mouse input is another essential aspect of game development, enabling players to interact with in-game elements. In this section, we will explore how to handle mouse input in your game using SFML.

1. Setting Up Mouse Input

To handle mouse input in SFML, you need to include the appropriate header and create an SFML `RenderWindow` object, similar to what we did for keyboard input. Here's a basic setup in C++:

```cpp
#include <SFML/Graphics.hpp>

int main() {
    sf::RenderWindow window(sf::VideoMode(800, 600), "SFML Mouse Input");

    while (window.isOpen()) {
        sf::Event event;
        while (window.pollEvent(event)) {
            if (event.type == sf::Event::Closed) {
                window.close();
            }
        }

        // Handle mouse input here

        window.clear();
        // Draw your game objects here
        window.display();
    }

    return 0;
}
```

2. Detecting Mouse Button Presses

SFML provides functions to detect mouse button presses. You can use the `sf::Mouse::isButtonPressed` function to check if a specific mouse button is currently pressed. For example, to check if the left mouse button is pressed:

```cpp
if (sf::Mouse::isButtonPressed(sf::Mouse::Left)) {
    // Left mouse button is currently pressed
}
```

3. Handling Mouse Button Releases

You can also detect when a mouse button is released using the `sf::Event` system. For instance, to detect when the right mouse button is released:

```
while (window.pollEvent(event)) {
    if (event.type == sf::Event::Closed) {
        window.close();
    }
    else if (event.type == sf::Event::MouseButtonReleased && event.mouseButto
n.button == sf::Mouse::Right) {
        // Right mouse button was released
    }
}
```

4. Getting Mouse Position

To interact with in-game elements based on mouse position, you can obtain the current mouse position relative to the game window. Here's how to retrieve the mouse position:

```
sf::Vector2i mousePosition = sf::Mouse::getPosition(window);
```

5. Handling Mouse Movement

Mouse movement can also be an important aspect of your game, especially for cursor-based interactions. You can track the mouse movement using the `sf::Event` system like this:

```
while (window.pollEvent(event)) {
    if (event.type == sf::Event::Closed) {
        window.close();
    }
    else if (event.type == sf::Event::MouseMoved) {
        // Mouse moved, event.mouseMove.x and event.mouseMove.y contain the n
ew position
    }
}
```

In summary, handling mouse input in your game allows players to interact with your game world, click on objects, and trigger various actions. SFML provides straightforward methods to detect mouse button presses, releases, mouse position, and movement, enabling you to create engaging and interactive gameplay experiences.

Section 12.3: Joystick and Gamepad Support

Joysticks and gamepads are common input devices for gaming, and SFML provides support for these devices to enhance the gaming experience. In this section, we'll explore how to handle joystick and gamepad input in your SFML game.

1. Detecting Connected Joysticks

SFML allows you to detect connected joysticks and gamepads. You can use the `sf::Joystick::isConnected` function to check if a specific joystick is connected. For example, to check if joystick number 0 is connected:

```cpp
if (sf::Joystick::isConnected(0)) {
    // Joystick 0 is connected
}
```

You can iterate through all the available joysticks to determine which ones are connected and provide appropriate support in your game.

2. Reading Joystick Axes

Joysticks typically have analog axes, such as thumbsticks or triggers. You can read the values of these axes using the `sf::Joystick::getAxisPosition` function. For example, to read the position of the X-axis (horizontal movement) of joystick 0:

```cpp
float xAxisPosition = sf::Joystick::getAxisPosition(0, sf::Joystick::X);
```

You can use these axis positions to control in-game elements, such as character movement or camera rotation.

3. Handling Joystick Buttons

Joysticks and gamepads come with buttons that you can use for various in-game actions. You can detect button presses using the `sf::Joystick::isButtonPressed` function. For instance, to check if button 0 of joystick 0 is pressed:

```cpp
if (sf::Joystick::isButtonPressed(0, 0)) {
    // Button 0 of joystick 0 is pressed
}
```

4. Polling Joystick Events

Similar to handling other input events in SFML, you can also poll joystick events using the `sf::Event` system. This allows you to capture joystick-related events in your game loop:

```cpp
sf::Event event;
while (window.pollEvent(event)) {
    if (event.type == sf::Event::JoystickButtonPressed) {
        // A joystick button was pressed
        unsigned int joystickID = event.joystickButton.joystickId;
        unsigned int button = event.joystickButton.button;
    }
    else if (event.type == sf::Event::JoystickMoved) {
        // A joystick axis was moved
        unsigned int joystickID = event.joystickMove.joystickId;
        sf::Joystick::Axis axis = event.joystickMove.axis;
        float position = event.joystickMove.position;
```

```
        }
}
```

5. Configuring Joystick Dead Zones

Joysticks and gamepads may have slight variations in their resting positions, leading to
unintended input. You can apply dead zones to joystick axes to ignore small variations. This
can be useful for improving control accuracy. Here's an example of setting a dead zone for
the X-axis of joystick 0:

```
sf::Joystick::setAxisThreshold(0, sf::Joystick::X, 15.0f); // Adjust the thre
shold value as needed
```

In summary, adding joystick and gamepad support to your SFML game enhances gameplay
by providing players with alternative input methods. SFML's joystick functions allow you to
detect connected devices, read axis positions, handle button presses, and configure dead
zones to ensure accurate and responsive controls for your game.

Section 12.4: Implementing Touchscreen Controls

In modern gaming, touchscreen controls have become prevalent, especially on mobile
devices. Implementing touchscreen controls in your SFML game allows you to cater to a
broader audience. This section explores how to integrate touchscreen controls seamlessly
into your game.

1. Detecting Touch Input

SFML provides easy ways to detect touch input on devices with touchscreens. You can use
the sf::Touch class to check if any fingers or touchpoints are currently touching the
screen:

```
if (sf::Touch::isDown(0)) {
    // At least one finger is touching the screen
}
```

You can replace 0 with the index of the finger you want to check if multiple fingers are
involved.

2. Reading Touch Positions

To retrieve the position of a touch or swipe, you can use the sf::Touch::getPosition
function. For example, to get the position of the first finger touch:

```
sf::Vector2i touchPosition = sf::Touch::getPosition(0);
```

You can then use these positions to interact with in-game elements, such as buttons or
character movement.

3. Handling Gestures

SFML also supports detecting various touch gestures, such as pinching, zooming, or swiping. You can utilize the `sf::Touch::Gesture` class to identify these gestures and respond accordingly. For instance, detecting a pinch gesture:

```
if (sf::Touch::Gesture::isPinchGesture(0)) {
    // Handle pinch gesture
}
```

4. Creating Touch-Based Controls

To implement touchscreen controls, you can create custom controls like virtual buttons or joysticks on the screen. These controls can be visual elements (e.g., sprites) that respond to touch input. Here's a basic example of creating a virtual button:

```
sf::RectangleShape button(sf::Vector2f(100, 50));
button.setFillColor(sf::Color::Green);
button.setPosition(50, 50);

// In your game loop:
if (sf::Touch::isDown(0)) {
    sf::Vector2i touchPosition = sf::Touch::getPosition(0);
    if (button.getGlobalBounds().contains(touchPosition.x, touchPosition.y))
{
        // The button was touched
        // Perform the corresponding action
    }
}
```

5. Multi-Touch Support

Modern devices often support multi-touch, meaning multiple fingers can interact with the screen simultaneously. SFML's touch input functions can handle multiple touchpoints, allowing you to create complex multi-touch interactions in your game.

In conclusion, implementing touchscreen controls in your SFML game expands its accessibility to a wider range of devices, including smartphones and tablets. You can detect touch input, read touch positions, handle gestures, and create custom touch-based controls to provide an intuitive and enjoyable gaming experience for touchscreen users.

Section 12.5: Custom Input Handling for Your Game

In many game development scenarios, you may need to implement custom input handling to tailor the user experience to your game's unique requirements. This section will guide you through the process of creating custom input handling for your SFML game.

1. Custom Key Bindings

SFML allows you to create custom key bindings, enabling players to configure their preferred keys for actions like movement, shooting, or opening menus. To implement custom key bindings, you can use data structures like `std::map` or `std::unordered_map` to map actions to key codes.

```cpp
// Define a map to store custom key bindings
std::unordered_map<Action, sf::Keyboard::Key> keyBindings;

// Initialize key bindings
keyBindings[Action::MoveLeft] = sf::Keyboard::A;
keyBindings[Action::MoveRight] = sf::Keyboard::D;
keyBindings[Action::Jump] = sf::Keyboard::Space;
```

In this example, `Action` is an enum representing different game actions.

2. Input Polling

To check for input in your game loop, you can use the `sf::Keyboard` and `sf::Mouse` classes to poll for key presses and mouse clicks. Here's an example of how to check if the "Jump" key is pressed:

```cpp
if (sf::Keyboard::isKeyPressed(keyBindings[Action::Jump])) {
    // Perform the jump action
}
```

3. Handling Continuous Input

For actions that require continuous input (e.g., holding a key to move continuously), you can use boolean flags to track the input state. Update these flags in your game loop based on input polling results.

```cpp
bool isMovingLeft = false;
bool isMovingRight = false;

if (sf::Keyboard::isKeyPressed(keyBindings[Action::MoveLeft])) {
    isMovingLeft = true;
}

if (sf::Keyboard::isKeyPressed(keyBindings[Action::MoveRight])) {
    isMovingRight = true;
}
```

4. Joystick and Gamepad Input

If your game supports game controllers, you can use the `sf::Joystick` class to handle input from joysticks and gamepads. You can check button presses, axis values, and other controller-specific input.

```cpp
// Check if button 0 (usually the "A" button) is pressed on joystick 0
if (sf::Joystick::isButtonPressed(0, 0)) {
    // Perform an action
}

// Read the position of the left joystick's X-axis
float xAxis = sf::Joystick::getAxisPosition(0, sf::Joystick::X);
```

5. Custom Input Events

For more complex input handling, you can create custom input events. SFML's event system allows you to define and trigger custom events. This can be useful for handling specific game interactions or user interface events.

```cpp
// Define a custom event type
sf::Event customEvent;
customEvent.type = sf::Event::EventType::CustomEventType;
customEvent.data1 = someData;
customEvent.data2 = otherData;

// Trigger the custom event
window.pushEvent(customEvent);
```

In your game loop, you can listen for these custom events and respond accordingly.

Custom input handling is essential for creating unique gameplay experiences and catering to player preferences. By implementing custom key bindings, input polling, continuous input tracking, joystick support, and custom input events, you can create a responsive and engaging gaming experience tailored to your game's design.

Chapter 13: Saving and Loading Game Data

In game development, the ability to save and load game data is crucial for providing players with a seamless gaming experience. This chapter explores various techniques and best practices for managing game saves, storing data in different formats, and ensuring the security of game data.

Section 13.1: Managing Game Saves

Game saves allow players to record their progress, high scores, and achievements, making it an integral part of many games. To manage game saves effectively, consider the following:

1. Save Slots

Implement multiple save slots, so players can have different save files for various playthroughs or profiles. This feature is especially useful for games with multiple story branches or game modes.

2. Save File Format

Choose an appropriate file format for your game saves. Common formats include JSON, XML, or binary files. JSON and XML offer human-readable formats, making it easier for players to edit save files manually, while binary files are more compact and efficient.

3. Auto-Saving

Implement an auto-save feature to periodically save the game's progress. Auto-saves ensure that players don't lose too much progress in case of unexpected game crashes or interruptions.

4. Checkpoint System

For games with levels or checkpoints, consider saving progress at these predefined points. This approach allows players to continue from specific milestones rather than starting from the beginning.

5. Player Preferences

Besides game progress, save and load player preferences such as audio settings, key bindings, and display options. This enhances the player experience by preserving their customized settings.

6. Encrypted Saves

To protect against save file manipulation, consider encrypting the save files. Encryption adds an additional layer of security, making it challenging for players to modify game data maliciously.

7. Cloud Saves

Offer cloud save functionality, allowing players to synchronize their progress across multiple devices. Services like Steam Cloud or third-party cloud providers can facilitate this feature.

8. Error Handling

Implement robust error handling for saving and loading processes. Provide informative error messages to players when issues arise, such as insufficient disk space or corrupted save files.

Here's an example of saving and loading game data using JSON in C++ with the help of the nlohmann/json library:

```cpp
#include <iostream>
#include <fstream>
#include <nlohmann/json.hpp>

using json = nlohmann::json;

// Function to save game data to a JSON file
void SaveGameData(const std::string& filename, const json& data) {
    std::ofstream file(filename);
    if (file.is_open()) {
        file << data.dump(4);   // Indented JSON for readability
        std::cout << "Game data saved to " << filename << std::endl;
    } else {
        std::cerr << "Error: Unable to save game data." << std::endl;
    }
    file.close();
}

// Function to load game data from a JSON file
json LoadGameData(const std::string& filename) {
    json data;
    std::ifstream file(filename);
    if (file.is_open()) {
        file >> data;
        std::cout << "Game data loaded from " << filename << std::endl;
    } else {
        std::cerr << "Error: Unable to load game data." << std::endl;
    }
    file.close();
    return data;
}

int main() {
    // Sample game data
    json gameData = {
```

```
        {"playerName", "Alice"},
        {"score", 1000},
        {"level", 5}
    };

    // Save game data to a file
    SaveGameData("save.json", gameData);

    // Load game data from the file
    json loadedData = LoadGameData("save.json");

    // Access loaded data
    std::cout << "Player Name: " << loadedData["playerName"] << std::endl;
    std::cout << "Score: " << loadedData["score"] << std::endl;
    std::cout << "Level: " << loadedData["level"] << std::endl;

    return 0;
}
```

This code snippet demonstrates a simple game data saving and loading mechanism using JSON in C++. You can adapt this approach to your game's specific data structure and file format.

Section 13.2: Using Text and Binary File I/O

In game development, managing game data often involves reading from and writing to files. Two common approaches for this purpose are using text files and binary files. Each has its advantages and use cases.

Text File I/O

Text files are human-readable and commonly used for storing game data in a format that can be easily edited. These files typically use plain text formats like JSON, XML, or custom-made formats. Here's an overview of using text file I/O in game development:

Pros:
1. **Human-Readable:** Text files are easy for both developers and players to read and modify manually. This makes debugging and customization more accessible.

2. **Compatibility:** Text files are platform-agnostic and can be read on various operating systems without compatibility issues.

3. **Debugging:** Debugging becomes more straightforward since you can inspect and modify text files with standard text editors.

Cons:
1. **Size:** Text files may be less space-efficient than binary files since they store data in a human-readable format, including whitespace and formatting.

2. **Parsing Overhead:** Reading and writing text files often require parsing, which can be slower than direct binary operations.

3. **Security:** Text files can be tampered with more easily since they are human-readable. Encryption is advisable for sensitive data.

Here's a simplified example of reading and writing game data using a text file in C++:

```cpp
#include <iostream>
#include <fstream>

// Function to save game data to a text file
void SaveGameData(const std::string& filename, const std::string& data) {
    std::ofstream file(filename);
    if (file.is_open()) {
        file << data;
        std::cout << "Game data saved to " << filename << std::endl;
    } else {
        std::cerr << "Error: Unable to save game data." << std::endl;
    }
    file.close();
}

// Function to load game data from a text file
std::string LoadGameData(const std::string& filename) {
    std::string data;
    std::ifstream file(filename);
    if (file.is_open()) {
        std::getline(file, data);
        std::cout << "Game data loaded from " << filename << std::endl;
    } else {
        std::cerr << "Error: Unable to load game data." << std::endl;
    }
    file.close();
    return data;
}

int main() {
    // Sample game data as a JSON string
    std::string gameData = R"({
        "playerName": "Bob",
        "score": 750,
        "level": 3
    })";

    // Save game data to a text file
```

```
SaveGameData("save.txt", gameData);

// Load game data from the text file
std::string loadedData = LoadGameData("save.txt");

// Access loaded data
std::cout << "Loaded Game Data: " << loadedData << std::endl;

return 0;
}
```

In this example, we use text file I/O to save and load game data stored as a JSON string. The data is read and written as plain text, making it easily modifiable and human-readable.

Binary File I/O

Binary files store data in a compact and efficient format that is not human-readable. They are commonly used when data size and speed are critical. Here are considerations for using binary file I/O in game development:

Pros:

1. **Efficiency:** Binary files are more space-efficient and faster to read and write than text files since they don't include formatting or human-readable characters.

2. **Security:** Binary files are harder to tamper with, as their contents are not human-readable. This provides a level of security for sensitive game data.

3. **Complex Data Structures:** Binary files are well-suited for saving complex data structures directly, without the need for serialization or parsing.

Cons:

1. **Debugging:** Debugging binary files can be challenging since their contents are not human-readable. Specialized tools are often required.

2. **Platform Dependency:** Binary files can have platform-specific data representations, potentially causing compatibility issues.

3. **Complexity:** Implementing binary file I/O may require more effort than text file I/O, particularly for custom binary formats.

Here's an example of reading and writing game data using a binary file in C++:

```cpp
#include <iostream>
#include <fstream>
#include <vector>

// Structure to represent game data
struct GameData {
    std::string playerName;
    int score;
```

```cpp
    int level;
};

// Function to save game data to a binary file
void SaveGameData(const std::string& filename, const GameData& data) {
    std::ofstream file(filename, std::ios::binary);
    if (file.is_open()) {
        file.write(reinterpret_cast<const char*>(&data), sizeof(GameData));
        std::cout << "Game data saved to " << filename
```

##
Section 13.3: Storing Game Data in JSON/XML

In modern game development, managing and storing game data is a crucial aspect. Game data can include player progress, level design, item properties, and more. Two commonly used formats for storing structured game data are JSON (JavaScript Object Notation) and XML (eXtensible Markup Language). In this section, we'll explore how to use JSON and XML to store and manage game data.

JSON (JavaScript Object Notation)

JSON is a lightweight data interchange format that is easy for humans to read and write and easy for machines to parse and generate. It's often used for configuration files, network communication, and, in our case, storing game data. JSON data is represented as key-value pairs, arrays, and nested objects.

Pros of Using JSON for Game Data:
1. **Human-Readable:** JSON is human-readable and easy to edit, which makes it a preferred choice for game data that may need manual adjustment during development.

2. **Platform-Agnostic:** JSON is platform-agnostic and can be used across various programming languages and platforms.

3. **Standardized:** JSON is a widely accepted format, and many programming languages have built-in support for parsing and generating JSON.

Here's an example of game data stored in JSON format:

```json
{
    "playerName": "Alice",
    "score": 1200,
    "inventory": [
        {
            "itemID": 1,
            "itemName": "Health Potion",
            "quantity": 5
        },
```

```
    {
        "itemID": 2,
        "itemName": "Sword",
        "quantity": 1
    }
  ]
}
```

In this example, we have game data that includes the player's name, score, and an inventory of items. The data is represented in a structured manner using JSON.

To work with JSON in your game, you'll need a JSON library appropriate for your programming language. Most modern languages have libraries that allow you to parse JSON strings into data structures and generate JSON from data structures.

XML (eXtensible Markup Language)

XML is another widely used format for storing structured data. It uses tags to define data elements and attributes to provide additional information about those elements. XML is commonly used for configuration files, data exchange, and sometimes for game data storage.

Pros of Using XML for Game Data:

1. **Structured:** XML enforces a clear structure on data, which can be beneficial for complex game data with many attributes and relationships.

2. **Self-Descriptive:** XML documents are self-descriptive, making it easier to understand the purpose of each data element.

3. **Schema Support:** XML can be validated against a schema, ensuring data integrity.

Here's an example of game data stored in XML format:

```
<playerData>
    <playerName>Alice</playerName>
    <score>1200</score>
    <inventory>
        <item>
            <itemID>1</itemID>
            <itemName>Health Potion</itemName>
            <quantity>5</quantity>
        </item>
        <item>
            <itemID>2</itemID>
            <itemName>Sword</itemName>
            <quantity>1</quantity>
        </item>
    </inventory>
</playerData>
```

In this XML example, we have similar game data to the JSON example. The data is structured hierarchically using XML elements and attributes.

To work with XML in your game, you'll need an XML parsing library appropriate for your programming language. Just like JSON, many languages offer libraries to handle XML data.

The choice between JSON and XML for storing game data depends on your project's specific requirements and the capabilities of your programming language. JSON is often preferred for its simplicity and human-readability, while XML may be a better choice for complex data structures that require strict validation. Consider your project's needs and the available libraries for your chosen programming language when making this decision.

In the next section, we'll explore how to implement game configuration files using JSON or XML and load them into your game.

Section 13.4: Implementing Game Configuration Files

Game configuration files are essential for controlling various aspects of your game without altering the source code. They allow you to adjust settings, tweak gameplay parameters, and make changes without recompiling the entire game. In this section, we'll discuss how to implement game configuration files using JSON or XML and load them into your game.

1. **Flexibility:** Configuration files provide a way to fine-tune your game without modifying the code. This flexibility is especially useful for game balancing, tweaking graphics settings, or adjusting gameplay rules.

2. **Ease of Maintenance:** Separating configuration data from code makes it easier to maintain and update your game. You can update settings without touching the codebase.

3. **Localization:** Configuration files can store text, allowing for easy localization and translation of your game.

JSON is a popular choice for game configuration files due to its simplicity and human-readability. Here's a basic example of a JSON configuration file for a game:

```
{
    "gameTitle": "My Awesome Game",
    "screenWidth": 1280,
    "screenHeight": 720,
    "soundVolume": 0.8,
    "difficulty": "medium"
}
```

In this example, we define settings like the game title, screen resolution, sound volume, and difficulty level. To implement JSON configuration files in your game, you'll need to:

1. **Load the JSON File:** Use a JSON library in your programming language to load the configuration file into memory.

2. **Parse the JSON Data:** Parse the JSON data into data structures or variables that your game code can access.

3. **Apply Configuration:** Use the parsed data to apply the game settings and parameters within your game code.

XML Configuration Files

XML is another option for configuration files, offering structured data storage. Here's an example of an XML configuration file:

```
<gameConfig>
    <gameTitle>My Awesome Game</gameTitle>
    <screenWidth>1280</screenWidth>
    <screenHeight>720</screenHeight>
    <soundVolume>0.8</soundVolume>
    <difficulty>medium</difficulty>
</gameConfig>
```

To implement XML configuration files in your game, follow these steps:

1. **Load the XML File:** Use an XML library in your programming language to load the configuration file.

2. **Parse the XML Data:** Parse the XML data into a format that your game code can work with.

3. **Apply Configuration:** Apply the parsed data to configure your game as needed.

Error Handling

When implementing configuration file loading and parsing, it's essential to include error handling. Files may not exist, or their structure may change over time. Proper error handling ensures that your game gracefully handles such situations.

Conclusion

Implementing game configuration files using JSON or XML provides a valuable tool for customizing and configuring your game. These files allow you to adjust settings, fine-tune gameplay, and even support localization without modifying your source code. By loading and parsing these files within your game, you can create a more flexible and maintainable gaming experience.

Section 13.5: Handling Data Encryption and Security

Data security is a crucial aspect of game development, especially when handling sensitive player data or preventing cheating. This section discusses various strategies for handling data encryption and security in your games.

Why Data Encryption?

Data encryption is the process of converting data into a code to prevent unauthorized access. In game development, encryption serves several purposes:

1. **Player Data Protection:** Encryption helps protect player information, such as login credentials, payment details, and personal data, from unauthorized access.

2. **Preventing Cheating:** Encryption can be used to secure game data to prevent cheating or tampering with saved game states and scores.

3. **Network Communication:** When your game communicates with servers or other players over the internet, encrypting data ensures that sensitive information is not intercepted or altered during transit.

Strategies for Data Encryption and Security

1. **User Authentication:** Implement secure user authentication mechanisms to ensure that only authorized users can access their accounts. Use industry-standard practices like salting and hashing passwords.

2. **Secure Communication:** When transmitting data over networks, use secure protocols like HTTPS for web-based games. For multiplayer games, implement secure socket layers (SSL) or transport layer security (TLS) for encrypted communication.

3. **Protecting Game Data:** Encrypt critical game data, such as saved game files or configuration files, to prevent cheating or tampering. Tools like symmetric or asymmetric encryption can be used.

4. **Secure Storage:** Store sensitive data securely on the client-side by utilizing secure storage mechanisms provided by the platform or operating system.

5. **Code Obfuscation:** Obfuscate your game's source code to make it harder for malicious actors to reverse engineer or tamper with it.

6. **Server-Side Validation:** Implement server-side validation for critical game actions, preventing cheating by validating game events on the server.

7. **Penetration Testing:** Regularly perform penetration testing and security audits to identify vulnerabilities and weaknesses in your game's security.

8.   **Regular Updates:** Keep your game and its dependencies up-to-date to patch security vulnerabilities. This includes game engines, libraries, and server software.

Encryption Algorithms

When implementing encryption in your game, choose appropriate encryption algorithms and key management practices. Common encryption algorithms include AES (Advanced Encryption Standard) for symmetric encryption and RSA for asymmetric encryption. Always use strong, well-established algorithms and keep keys secure.

Compliance with Data Regulations

If your game collects and stores user data, be aware of data protection regulations like the General Data Protection Regulation (GDPR) in Europe. Ensure that your game complies with these regulations, including obtaining user consent for data collection and providing mechanisms for data deletion.

Conclusion

Data encryption and security are essential aspects of modern game development, ensuring the protection of player data and the integrity of your game. By implementing encryption, secure communication, and following best practices for data security, you can create a more trustworthy and resilient gaming experience while safeguarding sensitive information.

Chapter 14: Networking and Multiplayer Games

In today's gaming landscape, multiplayer experiences have become increasingly popular. Whether you're developing a competitive eSport title or a cooperative adventure, networking and multiplayer functionality can significantly enhance your game's appeal. This chapter delves into the intricacies of networking in game development, allowing you to create engaging multiplayer experiences with the Simple and Fast Multimedia Library (SFML).

Section 14.1: Introduction to Networking in Game Development

Networking is the process of connecting multiple devices or computers to share data and resources. In game development, networking enables players to interact with each other in real-time, fostering competitive and cooperative experiences. Multiplayer games can be categorized into several types, including:

1.   **Local Multiplayer:** Players share a single physical location and use the same screen or device. This type includes split-screen gaming and games designed for local parties.

2. **Online Multiplayer:** Players connect over the internet, allowing for a global player base. Online multiplayer games can be further divided into various modes like cooperative, competitive, and massively multiplayer online (MMO) games.

3. **Asynchronous Multiplayer:** Players take turns and interact indirectly, often seen in games like Words with Friends or turn-based strategy games.

4. **LAN Multiplayer:** Players connect to a local area network (LAN) to enjoy multiplayer experiences within a confined space.

Networking in game development involves several key concepts:

- **Synchronization:** Ensuring that all players' game states are synchronized is crucial for a smooth multiplayer experience. This involves updating the game's state on all clients regularly.

- **Latency and Lag Compensation:** Network latency can lead to issues like lag. Game developers must implement mechanisms to compensate for these delays and provide a responsive experience.

- **Server-Client Model:** Many multiplayer games use a client-server model, where one player acts as the server, and others connect as clients. The server manages game state and enforces the rules.

- **P2P (Peer-to-Peer):** Some games use a peer-to-peer model, where all players have equal roles, and the game state is synchronized between them. P2P models are often used in small-scale multiplayer experiences.

In the context of SFML, you can implement networking using the built-in networking module, which supports both TCP and UDP protocols. TCP (Transmission Control Protocol) provides reliable, ordered, and error-checked data transmission, making it suitable for gameplay data. UDP (User Datagram Protocol) offers faster transmission but with the possibility of data loss or out-of-order packets, making it suitable for real-time updates like player positions.

In the following sections, we will explore how to set up networking in your SFML game, create a server-client architecture, and manage player interactions in both LAN and online multiplayer settings. You will learn the essentials needed to create engaging multiplayer games using SFML.

Section 14.2: Building Multiplayer Games with SFML

Building multiplayer games with SFML involves creating a networked environment where players can interact in real-time. To achieve this, you need to set up a server-client architecture, manage connections, and synchronize game states across all connected clients. This section will guide you through the essential steps of building multiplayer games using SFML.

Setting Up the Server-Client Architecture

In a multiplayer game, one player acts as the server, while others connect as clients. The server is responsible for maintaining the game state, handling player interactions, and broadcasting updates to all connected clients. Clients send input commands to the server and receive updates from it.

To set up the server-client architecture, you need to:

1. **Choose a Host:** Decide which player's machine will act as the server. It should have a stable internet connection and sufficient processing power to manage the game state and client connections.

2. **Create the Server:** Implement the server logic using SFML's `sf::TcpListener` and `sf::TcpSocket` classes. The server listens for incoming connections, accepts clients, and communicates game updates to them.

3. **Create the Client:** Develop the client application using SFML. Clients connect to the server, send input commands, and receive game updates from the server.

Managing Player Interactions

Player interactions in multiplayer games involve sending and receiving data between clients and the server. This data typically includes player positions, actions, and game events. SFML provides tools to facilitate this data exchange.

1. **Serialization:** To send and receive complex game data, you can use serialization techniques. Serialization involves converting game objects into a format that can be transmitted over the network and then deserialized on the other end. Popular serialization libraries, like Google's Protocol Buffers or JSON, are commonly used in game development.

2. **Input Commands:** Clients send input commands (e.g., move left, shoot) to the server, which processes them and updates the game state accordingly. The server then broadcasts the updated game state to all connected clients.

LAN vs. Online Multiplayer

SFML supports both LAN and online multiplayer. LAN multiplayer is suitable for local gaming sessions, where players connect to the same local network. Online multiplayer requires a dedicated server accessible via the internet, allowing players from different locations to join the game.

1. **LAN Multiplayer:** In LAN multiplayer, you can use the server's local IP address to connect clients. This approach is suitable for games intended to be played within a confined space, such as a LAN party.

2. **Online Multiplayer:** For online multiplayer, you need a publicly accessible server. Hosting services or cloud servers are common choices. Clients connect to the server using its public IP address or domain name.

Multiplayer games require security measures to prevent cheating and ensure a fair gaming experience. Implementing security features, such as data encryption, user authentication, and server-side validation of player actions, is essential to maintain game integrity.

In this section, you have gained an overview of building multiplayer games with SFML. Setting up the server-client architecture, managing player interactions, and considering LAN vs. online multiplayer are fundamental aspects of creating engaging multiplayer experiences. In the following sections, we will explore more advanced topics, including online leaderboards, chat systems, and server-client communication strategies.

Section 14.3: Creating Online Leaderboards

Online leaderboards are a popular feature in multiplayer games that allow players to compete with each other and showcase their achievements. Implementing online leaderboards in your SFML game can enhance player engagement and provide a competitive edge. In this section, we'll explore how to create online leaderboards for your multiplayer game.

Database Integration

The backbone of any online leaderboard system is a database that stores player scores and other relevant information. You can use a variety of database systems, including MySQL, PostgreSQL, or NoSQL databases like MongoDB, depending on your project's requirements.

1. **Design the Database Schema:** Define the structure of your leaderboard database, including tables for players, scores, and any additional data you want to store. Consider using an Object-Relational Mapping (ORM) library to interact with the database from your game code.

2. **Database Connection:** Establish a connection to the database server from your game server. You'll need to configure database credentials and connection settings.

3. **Inserting Scores:** When a player achieves a high score, the game server should insert the score record into the database. Include the player's ID or username, the achieved score, and a timestamp.

Retrieving and Displaying Leaderboards

Once scores are stored in the database, you can retrieve and display leaderboards within the game client. Here's how to do it:

1. **Querying Scores:** Write SQL queries to retrieve the top scores from the database. You can order scores by the highest score value and limit the results to the top N players.

2. **API or Web Service:** Consider exposing an API or web service that the game client can use to request leaderboard data. This allows for flexibility if you want to create web-based leaderboards or support multiple game clients (e.g., mobile and desktop).

3. **Leaderboard Display:** In the game client, create a leaderboard screen or UI element that displays the top players and their scores. You can use SFML's graphical capabilities to create a visually appealing leaderboard.

Security and Fairness

Online leaderboards should be secure and fair. To achieve this:

1. **Authentication:** Ensure that only authenticated players can submit scores to the leaderboard. Implement user account systems with secure authentication mechanisms.

2. **Cheating Prevention:** Implement measures to prevent cheating, such as validating submitted scores on the server side and using anti-cheat algorithms. Regularly monitor the leaderboard for suspicious activity.

3. **Data Privacy:** Respect players' privacy by adhering to data protection regulations, such as GDPR. Inform players about data collection practices and allow them to opt out if desired.

Real-Time Updates

For a dynamic and engaging experience, consider implementing real-time updates to the leaderboard. Notify players when their scores change or when they achieve a new rank.

1. **WebSocket or Push Notifications:** Use technologies like WebSockets or push notifications to send updates to players' game clients when there are changes to the leaderboard.

2. **Periodic Updates:** Periodically refresh the leaderboard data in the game client, ensuring that players always have up-to-date information.

Creating online leaderboards adds a competitive and social dimension to your multiplayer game. Players can strive to achieve top rankings and compete with others, enhancing their gaming experience. When designing leaderboards, prioritize data security, fairness, and real-time updates to provide a compelling and engaging feature.

Section 14.4: Implementing Chat Systems

In online multiplayer games, communication among players is crucial for teamwork, strategizing, or simply socializing. Implementing a chat system allows players to interact with each other in real-time. In this section, we'll explore how to implement a chat system for your multiplayer SFML game.

Components of a Chat System

A chat system typically consists of the following components:

1. **Chat Interface:** The user interface for sending and receiving messages. This interface can be displayed within the game client, often as a chatbox or overlay.

2. **Server-Side Logic:** The game server manages incoming and outgoing messages, enforces chat rules, and broadcasts messages to appropriate recipients.

3. **Networking:** Communication between the game client and server is necessary to relay messages. You can use sockets or a networking library like SFML's `sf::TcpSocket` for this purpose.

Server-Side Chat Logic

Here's how to implement server-side chat logic:

1. **Message Handling:** Define message structures that include the sender's ID or username, the message content, and a timestamp. When a player sends a message, the server validates it, attaches necessary information, and stores it temporarily.

2. **Message Broadcast:** The server broadcasts messages to relevant recipients, such as players within the same game room or those on a friend list. Implement logic to determine who should receive each message.

3. **Chat Commands:** Allow players to send special commands, such as "/whisper" for private messages or "/mute" to mute specific users. Parse incoming messages for these commands and execute the appropriate actions.

Client-Side Chat Interface

Implementing the chat interface in the game client involves the following steps:

1. **User Input:** Capture user input for sending messages. Players typically press a key to open the chatbox and enter messages. Use SFML's input handling capabilities to detect keypresses.

2. **Display Messages:** Create a graphical interface element, such as a chatbox or chat window, to display messages. New messages should appear at the bottom, and older messages should be scrollable.

3. **Formatting:** Allow for text formatting options like color-coding messages, custom fonts, and emoji support to enhance the chat's visual appeal.

4. **Scrolling:** Implement scrolling functionality so that players can view older messages as the chat history grows.

Security and Moderation

To maintain a safe and enjoyable gaming environment, consider these security and moderation aspects:

1. **Profanity Filter:** Implement a profanity filter to automatically censor or block offensive language. Be cautious not to over-censor, as false positives can frustrate players.

2. **Report System:** Allow players to report inappropriate behavior or messages. Create a system for handling these reports and taking necessary actions against offenders.

3. **Anti-Spam Measures:** Implement anti-spam measures to prevent flooding the chat with messages. You can use rate limiting or cooldowns between messages.

Real-Time Updates

For real-time chat interactions, you can use WebSockets or a similar technology to enable instant message delivery. This ensures that players can communicate seamlessly and without delays.

Integration with Player Accounts

For a more personalized experience, consider integrating the chat system with player accounts. This allows players to have unique usernames, maintain friends lists, and manage their chat preferences.

Implementing a chat system enhances player engagement and fosters a sense of community in your multiplayer SFML game. It's a valuable feature for both cooperative and competitive gameplay, allowing players to strategize, socialize, and share their gaming experiences.

Section 14.5: Handling Server and Client Communication

In online multiplayer games, efficient communication between the game server and clients is crucial for ensuring smooth gameplay and synchronization of game states. This section explores the techniques and considerations for handling server and client communication in an SFML-based multiplayer game.

Client-Server Architecture

Most multiplayer games use a client-server architecture, where there are two main components: the game server and the game clients (players). The server acts as the authoritative source of game state and handles game logic, while clients render the game and send input to the server. Communication between clients and the server is essential for keeping everyone in sync.

Networking Libraries

SFML provides networking capabilities through the `sf::TcpSocket` and `sf::TcpListener` classes, which are suitable for basic client-server communication. However, for more complex multiplayer games, you may want to consider using dedicated networking libraries or frameworks, such as RakNet, ENet, or Boost.Asio, which offer features like packet management, reliability, and latency optimization.

Sending and Receiving Data

To exchange data between the server and clients, you'll need to define a protocol that specifies how messages are structured and transmitted. This includes defining message types, serialization, and deserialization methods.

When sending data, serialize the game state or messages into a byte stream before transmission. On the receiving end, deserialize the received data to extract meaningful information. Serialization libraries like Google's Protocol Buffers or JSON can simplify this process.

Message Types

In a multiplayer game, various types of messages need to be exchanged between the server and clients:

1. **Game State Updates:** The server sends updates about the game world, including player positions, object states, and events. Clients need to process these updates to render the game accurately.

2. **Player Input:** Clients send player input (e.g., key presses, mouse clicks) to the server, which processes the input and updates the game state accordingly.

3. **Chat Messages:** If your game includes a chat system (as discussed in previous sections), chat messages need to be exchanged between players through the server.

4. **Events and Notifications:** Important events, such as a player's death or a new player joining the game, should be communicated to all clients for synchronization.

Latency and Prediction

Network latency is a common challenge in multiplayer games. To mitigate its effects, consider implementing client-side prediction and server reconciliation. Client-side prediction allows the client to simulate game state locally based on input while waiting for the server's response. Server reconciliation then corrects any discrepancies between the client's simulation and the authoritative server state.

Bandwidth Optimization

Minimizing the amount of data sent over the network can reduce bandwidth usage and improve performance. Techniques for bandwidth optimization include delta compression (sending only changes in game state) and interpolation (smoothing out updates for smoother rendering).

Security and Anti-Cheating Measures

Multiplayer games are susceptible to cheating and hacking. Implement security measures to protect against cheating, such as server-side validation of player actions and detecting unusual behavior patterns. Additionally, encryption and authentication protocols can help secure communication between clients and the server.

Handling server and client communication is a fundamental aspect of multiplayer game development with SFML. A well-designed communication system ensures that players have a consistent and enjoyable experience while playing together, even when faced with challenges like network latency and potential cheating.

Chapter 15: Optimizing Your SFML Game

Section 15.1: Performance Profiling and Benchmarking

In the world of game development, performance optimization plays a crucial role in delivering a smooth and enjoyable gaming experience to players. Performance issues can lead to frame rate drops, input lag, and other undesirable effects that can detract from the immersion of your game. To address these challenges, it's essential to utilize performance profiling and benchmarking techniques to identify bottlenecks and areas for improvement in your SFML game.

Performance profiling involves analyzing your game's execution to pinpoint specific functions or code sections that consume a significant amount of computational resources, such as CPU time or memory. Once identified, these performance bottlenecks can be optimized to enhance your game's overall performance. Let's explore some essential aspects of performance profiling and benchmarking in the context of SFML game development.

Understanding Profiling Tools

Profiling tools are specialized software applications designed to monitor and analyze the behavior of your game during runtime. They provide insights into which parts of your code are the most time-consuming or memory-intensive. Some popular profiling tools for C++ and SFML development include:

- **Valgrind**: Valgrind is a memory analysis tool that can help you identify memory leaks and inefficient memory usage in your SFML application.

- **gprof**: The GNU Profiler (gprof) is a widely-used profiling tool for analyzing CPU usage. It can generate a profile of function call times and help you identify performance bottlenecks in your code.

- **SFML Profiler**: SFML itself provides a built-in profiling system that you can use to measure the time spent in specific parts of your code.

Profiling Your SFML Game

To start profiling your SFML game, follow these general steps:

1. **Instrument Your Code**: To use a profiler effectively, you'll need to instrument your code by adding profiling commands or annotations. Profiling tools work by tracking these markers to measure the execution time of specific code sections.

2. **Run the Profiler**: Launch your game under the control of the profiling tool. Let it run for a while to gather data.

3. **Analyze the Results**: After your game session, the profiler generates reports and statistics that highlight performance bottlenecks. These reports often include information about CPU usage, memory allocation, and function call times.

4. **Optimize Your Code**: Armed with profiling data, you can identify areas of your code that require optimization. This might involve optimizing algorithms, reducing memory allocations, or parallelizing computationally intensive tasks.

Benchmarking Your SFML Game

Benchmarking is another essential technique for assessing the performance of your SFML game. Unlike profiling, which focuses on identifying bottlenecks in existing code, benchmarking involves creating controlled tests to measure the performance of specific functions or algorithms under different conditions.

To implement benchmarking in your SFML game:

1. **Identify Critical Components**: Determine which parts of your game code are critical for performance. These might include rendering, physics calculations, or AI routines.

2. **Design Benchmark Tests**: Create benchmark tests that isolate and measure the performance of these components. For example, you could measure the time it takes to render a certain number of sprites or process a specific number of AI calculations.

3. **Collect Benchmark Data**: Run your benchmark tests under various conditions, such as different hardware configurations or load levels. Collect data on execution times and other relevant metrics.

4. **Analyze Benchmark Results**: Analyze the benchmark results to identify performance trends and bottlenecks. Use this information to optimize the critical components of your game.

Remember that performance optimization is an iterative process. After making changes to your code, it's essential to re-run your profiling and benchmarking tests to verify the effectiveness of your optimizations. Additionally, consider the trade-offs between performance and maintainability, as some optimizations may make your code more complex.

In the next sections, we will delve deeper into memory management techniques, GPU acceleration, and other strategies to optimize your SFML game further. These optimizations will help ensure that your game runs smoothly on a wide range of hardware configurations, providing an enjoyable experience to players.

Section 15.2: Memory Management Techniques

Efficient memory management is a critical aspect of optimizing your SFML game. Inefficient memory usage can lead to performance issues, such as frame rate drops and increased loading times. In this section, we'll explore memory management techniques that can help you reduce memory overhead and improve the overall performance of your game.

1. Object Pooling

Object pooling is a technique used to manage memory more efficiently, especially when dealing with frequently created and destroyed objects. In an SFML game, this can be particularly useful for managing entities like bullets, particles, or enemies.

Here's how object pooling works:

- Instead of creating and destroying objects as needed, you preallocate a pool of objects during game initialization.
- When you need an object, you take one from the pool, use it, and return it to the pool when it's no longer needed.
- This reduces the overhead of frequent object creation and destruction, resulting in smoother performance.

```cpp
// Example of a simple object pool for bullets
class Bullet {
    // ...
};

class BulletPool {
public:
    BulletPool(int poolSize) {
        for (int i = 0; i < poolSize; ++i) {
            bullets.emplace_back(std::make_unique<Bullet>());
        }
    }

    Bullet* getBullet() {
        for (auto& bullet : bullets) {
            if (!bullet->isActive()) {
                bullet->reset(); // Initialize the bullet's state
                return bullet.get();
            }
        }
        return nullptr; // No available bullets
    }

private:
    std::vector<std::unique_ptr<Bullet>> bullets;
};
```

2. Texture and Resource Management

Loading and unloading textures, sounds, and other game resources can impact performance and memory usage. Implement a resource management system to handle resources efficiently:

- Load resources once during initialization and keep them in memory.
- Unload resources that are no longer needed (e.g., when transitioning between game levels).
- Reuse resources whenever possible to avoid redundant loading.

SFML provides resource management classes like `sf::Texture`, which can help you efficiently load and manage textures.

3. Smart Pointers

Smart pointers, such as `std::shared_ptr` and `std::unique_ptr`, can assist in managing memory effectively and preventing memory leaks. They automatically handle the destruction of objects when they are no longer referenced.

```
std::shared_ptr<sf::Texture> texture = std::make_shared<sf::Texture>();
// Use the texture...
// When it's no longer needed, it will be automatically deallocated.
```

4. Texture Atlases

Texture atlases involve combining multiple images into a single texture, reducing the number of texture switches and improving rendering performance. Use tools like TexturePacker or ShoeBox to create texture atlases for your game assets.

5. Profile and Optimize

Profiling tools, as mentioned in the previous section, can help you identify memory-related issues in your game. Pay attention to memory leaks, excessive memory allocations, and large memory buffers that may not be necessary.

Optimize data structures to reduce memory overhead. Consider using smaller data types or custom data structures that better fit the specific needs of your game.

By implementing these memory management techniques, you can minimize memory-related performance issues and create a more responsive and efficient SFML game. Keep in mind that efficient memory management is an ongoing process, and regular profiling and optimization are essential for maintaining optimal performance as your game evolves.

Section 15.3: GPU Acceleration and OpenGL Integration

Utilizing the power of the Graphics Processing Unit (GPU) is crucial for achieving high-performance graphics in your SFML game. SFML provides ways to integrate with OpenGL, a low-level graphics API, allowing you to leverage hardware acceleration for rendering. In this section, we'll explore GPU acceleration and OpenGL integration techniques.

1. Understanding OpenGL

OpenGL is a widely-used graphics API that provides direct access to the GPU. SFML uses OpenGL under the hood for its rendering. To harness the full potential of the GPU, you need to understand the basics of OpenGL.

- OpenGL is a state machine: You set various states (e.g., blending, shaders, textures) and then issue draw commands to render objects.
- Shaders: Shaders are small programs executed on the GPU. Vertex shaders manipulate vertex data, while fragment shaders determine pixel colors. SFML allows you to write your shaders for advanced rendering effects.
- VBOs and VAOs: Vertex Buffer Objects (VBOs) and Vertex Array Objects (VAOs) allow you to efficiently store and render vertex data on the GPU.

2. Integrating Custom OpenGL Code

SFML provides a way to integrate custom OpenGL code into your application. You can access the OpenGL context through the `sf::Window` class.

Here's a basic example of initializing OpenGL within SFML:

```cpp
sf::Window window(sf::VideoMode(800, 600), "SFML OpenGL");

// Initialize OpenGL
if (glewInit() != GLEW_OK) {
    std::cerr << "Failed to initialize GLEW" << std::endl;
    return -1;
}

// Define and compile shaders
const char* vertexShaderSource = "your_vertex_shader_code";
const char* fragmentShaderSource = "your_fragment_shader_code";
GLuint vertexShader, fragmentShader, shaderProgram;

// Create and compile the vertex shader
vertexShader = glCreateShader(GL_VERTEX_SHADER);
glShaderSource(vertexShader, 1, &vertexShaderSource, NULL);
glCompileShader(vertexShader);

// Create and compile the fragment shader
fragmentShader = glCreateShader(GL_FRAGMENT_SHADER);
glShaderSource(fragmentShader, 1, &fragmentShaderSource, NULL);
glCompileShader(fragmentShader);

// Create a shader program and link the shaders
shaderProgram = glCreateProgram();
```

```
glAttachShader(shaderProgram, vertexShader);
glAttachShader(shaderProgram, fragmentShader);
glLinkProgram(shaderProgram);
glUseProgram(shaderProgram);

// Render Loop
while (window.isOpen()) {
    // Clear the screen
    glClear(GL_COLOR_BUFFER_BIT);

    // Render your OpenGL content here

    // Display the result
    window.display();
}
```

3. Mixing SFML and OpenGL

You can combine SFML's high-level features with custom OpenGL rendering. For example, you can use SFML to create a window, handle user input, and manage resources, while using OpenGL for advanced rendering effects.

4. GPU-Friendly Data Structures

To maximize GPU performance, use data structures that are GPU-friendly. For example, use VBOs and VAOs to store vertex data efficiently. Minimize CPU-GPU data transfers, as they can be a bottleneck.

5. Profiling and Optimizing

Profile your game using GPU profiling tools to identify performance bottlenecks. Optimizing OpenGL code may involve reducing draw calls, optimizing shaders, and minimizing state changes.

In summary, understanding OpenGL and GPU acceleration is essential for achieving high-performance graphics in your SFML game. By integrating custom OpenGL code and optimizing GPU-related operations, you can unlock the full potential of modern graphics hardware for your game's visuals.

Section 15.4: Reducing Input Lag

Input lag, the delay between a player's input and the corresponding on-screen action, can significantly impact the gaming experience. Minimizing input lag is crucial for creating responsive and enjoyable games. In this section, we'll explore techniques to reduce input lag in your SFML game.

1. Understanding Input Lag

Input lag can be caused by various factors:

- **Polling Rate**: The frequency at which you check for input events affects input responsiveness. Ensure you're polling input devices (e.g., keyboard, mouse) frequently enough to capture rapid inputs.

- **Frame Rate**: The frame rate at which your game runs affects input lag. Higher frame rates generally result in lower input lag. Aim for a smooth and consistent frame rate.

- **Input Processing**: How you handle input events can introduce lag. For example, if you delay input processing until the end of a frame, there will be a noticeable delay.

2. Implementing Low-Latency Input

To reduce input lag, consider the following techniques:

- **Input Polling**: Poll input devices (e.g., sf::Keyboard, sf::Mouse) at the beginning of each frame to minimize input processing delay.

- **Frame Rate Independence**: Design your game to be frame rate independent. This means that game logic should advance by a fixed time step, regardless of the frame rate. This prevents input lag from varying frame rates.

```cpp
sf::Clock clock;
const sf::Time timePerFrame = sf::seconds(1.0f / 60.0f); // 60 FPS

while (window.isOpen()) {
    sf::Time deltaTime = clock.restart();

    // Poll input
    sf::Event event;
    while (window.pollEvent(event)) {
        // Handle input events
    }

    // Update game logic with a fixed time step
    update(deltaTime);

    // Render the frame
    render();
}
```

- **Triple Buffering**: Triple buffering can help reduce input lag by providing a smoother frame rate. It involves having three frame buffers: one for rendering, one for display, and one for input. Implementing this technique can be complex but can be worthwhile for demanding games.

3. Reducing GPU Load

High GPU load can introduce input lag. To mitigate this:

- Optimize your rendering pipeline to reduce GPU rendering time. Avoid overdraw, minimize shader complexity, and batch rendering where possible.

- Monitor GPU performance using profiling tools to identify bottlenecks.

- Implement a GPU-friendly update mechanism to avoid stalling the CPU-GPU pipeline.

- Minimize CPU-GPU synchronization, as it can introduce stalls.

- Ensure your game's resource management (e.g., textures, shaders) is efficient to avoid GPU thrashing.

4. Consistent User Experience

Maintaining a consistent frame rate is essential for a smooth gaming experience. If your game cannot maintain a high frame rate, consider limiting the frame rate to a consistent value to avoid fluctuations that can lead to perceived input lag.

5. User Feedback

Finally, gather feedback from players to identify and address input lag issues. Different players may have varying tolerance levels for input lag, so user feedback is invaluable for fine-tuning your game's responsiveness.

In conclusion, minimizing input lag is crucial for creating responsive and enjoyable games. By understanding the factors that contribute to input lag and implementing techniques such as low-latency input handling, frame rate independence, and GPU optimization, you can provide players with a smoother and more immersive gaming experience.

Section 15.5: Achieving Smooth Gameplay

Achieving smooth gameplay is a critical aspect of game development. Players expect a consistent and enjoyable experience without interruptions or slowdowns. In this section, we'll explore techniques to optimize your SFML game for smooth gameplay.

1. Maintain a Consistent Frame Rate

A consistent frame rate is key to smooth gameplay. Frame rate fluctuations can result in jitters and affect the player's experience negatively. To maintain a consistent frame rate:

- Use a fixed time step for your game's logic. This ensures that game updates occur at a predictable rate, regardless of the frame rate. Here's an example:

```
sf::Clock clock;
const sf::Time timePerFrame = sf::seconds(1.0f / 60.0f); // 60 FPS

while (window.isOpen()) {
    sf::Time deltaTime = clock.restart();

    // Update game logic with a fixed time step
    update(deltaTime);

    // Render the frame
    render();

    // Cap the frame rate
    sf::sleep(timePerFrame - clock.getElapsedTime());
}
```

- Profile and optimize your game to ensure it can consistently achieve the target frame rate. Identify performance bottlenecks and optimize resource-intensive code.

2. Efficient Resource Management

Efficient management of game resources such as textures, sounds, and shaders is crucial for smooth gameplay:

- Load and unload resources dynamically as needed. Avoid keeping all resources in memory simultaneously, as it can lead to excessive memory usage and slowdowns.

- Implement resource caching to reuse loaded resources efficiently. This minimizes disk I/O and loading times.

- Compress and optimize textures and assets to reduce memory usage and loading times.

3. GPU Optimization

Optimizing GPU usage is essential for smooth rendering:

- Minimize overdraw by sorting and batching rendering operations. Avoid rendering objects that are not visible.

- Use efficient shaders and rendering techniques. Complex shaders can impact GPU performance.

- Implement occlusion culling to skip rendering of objects that are not visible to the camera.

4. Memory Management

Proper memory management is critical for preventing memory-related slowdowns:

- Profile your game's memory usage and address memory leaks or excessive allocations.

- Use object pooling for frequently created and destroyed objects to reduce memory allocation overhead.

- Optimize data structures and minimize unnecessary copying of data.

5. Input Lag Reduction

Reducing input lag enhances gameplay responsiveness:

- Poll input devices (e.g., keyboard, mouse) at the beginning of each frame to minimize input processing delay.

- Implement frame rate independence, ensuring that game logic advances by a fixed time step.

- Optimize the input handling code to reduce latency between user input and in-game actions.

6. Threading and Parallelism

Consider using multithreading and parallelism to distribute computational load:

- Offload non-rendering tasks (e.g., AI calculations, physics simulations) to worker threads to prevent the main thread from getting blocked.

- Ensure proper synchronization to avoid race conditions and data conflicts.

7. Profiling and Benchmarking

Regularly profile and benchmark your game to identify performance bottlenecks. Profiling tools can help pinpoint areas that require optimization. Continuously monitor and fine-tune your game's performance throughout development.

8. Testing on Target Hardware

Test your game on the target hardware to ensure it runs smoothly on various configurations. What performs well on one system may not perform the same on another.

In conclusion, achieving smooth gameplay in your SFML game involves optimizing frame rate, resource management, GPU usage, memory management, input lag, and leveraging threading when necessary. Regular profiling and testing on target hardware are essential to identify and address performance issues. By following these guidelines, you can provide players with a consistent and enjoyable gaming experience.

Chapter 16: Publishing Your Game

Section 16.1: Preparing Your Game for Distribution

Publishing your game is the final step in the game development process. It involves preparing your game for distribution to players. Whether you plan to release your game on a game platform, app store, or your website, there are several key considerations and steps you should follow to ensure a successful game launch. In this section, we'll focus on preparing your game for distribution.

1. Final Testing and Quality Assurance

Before you release your game to the public, thorough testing and quality assurance (QA) are crucial. Test your game extensively to identify and fix any remaining bugs, glitches, or balance issues. Conduct QA testing on various devices and platforms to ensure compatibility.

2. Performance Optimization

Optimize your game's performance to ensure it runs smoothly on a wide range of hardware configurations. Consider the following:

- **System Requirements:** Clearly define the minimum and recommended system requirements for your game. This information helps potential players determine if their systems can run your game.

- **Graphics Settings:** Provide in-game graphics settings that allow players to adjust quality levels (e.g., graphics detail, resolution, anti-aliasing) to suit their hardware.

3. User Interface (UI) Polish

Polish the game's user interface to provide an intuitive and enjoyable user experience. Ensure that menus, buttons, and controls are easy to navigate. Implement accessibility features to accommodate players with disabilities.

4. Licensing and Legal Compliance

Review and comply with all legal requirements and licensing agreements. Ensure that your game doesn't infringe on copyrights, trademarks, or patents. If your game uses third-party assets or libraries, verify that you have the necessary licenses and permissions.

5. Localization

If you plan to release your game in multiple regions, invest in localization. Translate in-game text, subtitles, and audio to accommodate players from different linguistic backgrounds. Consider cultural adaptations and sensitivities in your game content.

6. Game Documentation

Prepare comprehensive game documentation, including user manuals, installation guides, and troubleshooting instructions. Clear documentation can help players resolve issues and enhance their gaming experience.

7. Playtesting and Feedback

Conduct playtesting sessions with a group of beta testers to gather feedback. Beta testing allows you to identify issues you might have missed and make final adjustments based on player input.

8. Marketing and Promotion

Plan your game's marketing and promotional strategy well in advance of the release date. Consider the following marketing activities:

- **Press Releases:** Write and distribute press releases to gaming news websites and blogs.

- **Social Media:** Build a strong presence on social media platforms to engage with your audience and generate interest.

- **Trailer and Screenshots:** Create an appealing game trailer and screenshots to showcase your game's features.

- **Community Engagement:** Interact with gaming communities, forums, and discussion boards related to your game's genre.

- **Demo or Early Access:** Consider releasing a demo or an early access version of your game to generate buzz and gather player feedback.

9. Distribution Platforms

Choose the distribution platforms that align with your game's target audience. Options include app stores (e.g., Steam, Epic Games Store, Apple App Store), your own website, or console-specific platforms (e.g., PlayStation Network, Xbox Live).

10. Pre-Release Checklist

Before you hit the publish button, create a pre-release checklist to ensure everything is in order. This checklist should include tasks like:

- Verifying that all assets are correctly packaged.
- Testing the installer or distribution method.
- Double-checking that the game's licensing and legal documentation is included.
- Ensuring that your marketing materials are ready to go.

Once your game is live, monitor its performance, gather player feedback, and be prepared to release updates and patches. Providing ongoing support and updates demonstrates your commitment to the player community and can help maintain a positive reputation.

By following these steps and carefully preparing your game for distribution, you can increase your game's chances of success in the competitive world of game development. Remember that effective marketing, player engagement, and post-launch support are essential for the long-term success of your game.

Section 16.2: Packaging Game Assets

Packaging game assets is a critical aspect of preparing your game for distribution. Properly organizing and bundling your game's assets ensures that everything is ready for players to enjoy. In this section, we'll explore the key considerations for packaging your game assets effectively.

Asset Organization

Before you package your game assets, organize them systematically. A well-structured asset hierarchy makes it easier to manage and maintain your game. Consider the following organization tips:

- **Folders by Type:** Group assets (e.g., textures, sounds, models) into separate folders for clarity.

- **Subfolders:** If you have many assets of the same type, create subfolders within each type folder to further categorize them.

- **Naming Conventions:** Use consistent and descriptive file and folder names to make assets easy to locate.

- **Version Control:** If you're using version control software like Git, ensure that your asset folders are properly integrated into your repository.

Asset Compression

To reduce the overall size of your game package, consider compressing assets where appropriate. Many image, audio, and video formats support compression without sacrificing quality. Utilize tools and libraries that can help automate this process during the packaging stage.

Resource Management

Implement a resource management system to efficiently load and unload assets during gameplay. This system helps minimize memory usage and loading times. You can use libraries like SFML's resource management system or develop a custom solution tailored to your game's needs.

Asset Packaging Tools

Depending on your game's platform and distribution method, you may need specific asset packaging tools. These tools help bundle assets into a format suitable for distribution. For example:

- **Unity**: Unity provides built-in asset packaging features that allow you to define asset bundles for different platforms.

- **Unreal Engine**: Unreal Engine's Packaging Wizard assists in preparing game builds for various platforms.

- **CMake**: If you're using CMake to manage your project, you can create custom packaging scripts to handle asset bundling.

Compression Formats

Consider using appropriate compression formats for different asset types:

- **Textures**: Use formats like PNG or JPEG for images. These formats provide a good balance between quality and file size.

- **Audio**: Compress audio files using formats like MP3 or Ogg Vorbis, which offer high-quality compression.

- **Video**: If your game includes video assets, use codecs like H.264 for efficient compression.

Asset Encryption

To protect your game's assets from unauthorized access or tampering, consider encrypting them. Encryption ensures that assets are only accessible to your game's code. Implement encryption and decryption routines in your game engine or use third-party libraries for this purpose.

Platform-Specific Considerations

Different platforms may have specific requirements for asset packaging. Be sure to consult the documentation and guidelines provided by the platform(s) you intend to release your game on. For example, console platforms like PlayStation and Xbox may have strict asset packaging and encryption requirements.

Packaging Validation

Before finalizing your game package, validate it thoroughly. Ensure that all assets are correctly bundled, and the game runs as expected. Test the installation process on different target platforms to identify and address any issues that may arise during installation or asset loading.

Backup and Versioning

Maintain backups of your packaged game assets and create version snapshots. This practice helps you revert to previous versions in case of issues with updates or patches. Utilize version control systems like Git to track changes in your assets over time.

Properly packaging your game assets is a crucial step in ensuring a smooth and successful game launch. Organize, compress, and protect your assets while following platform-specific guidelines to provide players with the best possible gaming experience. Remember that efficient asset packaging contributes to faster loading times and optimized resource management, enhancing the overall quality of your game.

Section 16.3: Building and Distributing Your Game

Once your game is ready for distribution, the next step is to build and package it for various platforms and distribution channels. This section covers the essential considerations for building and distributing your game effectively.

Building Game Executables

Building game executables involves compiling your source code and assets into a format that players can run. The exact process varies depending on your game engine and platform. Here are some key points to keep in mind:

- **Compile for Multiple Platforms**: If you're targeting multiple platforms (e.g., Windows, macOS, Linux), you'll need to build separate executables for each. Utilize cross-compilation tools or platform-specific development environments.

- **Compile for Different Architectures**: Consider the architecture of the target devices (e.g., x86, x64, ARM) and compile your game accordingly. This is especially important for mobile platforms.

- **Debug and Release Builds**: Create both debug and release builds of your game. Debug builds include debugging information for troubleshooting, while release builds are optimized for performance and have smaller file sizes.

- **Dependencies and Libraries**: Ensure that all required libraries and dependencies are included with your game executable. This may involve static linking or bundling necessary libraries.

Packaging Game Assets

As discussed in Section 16.2, packaging game assets is a critical step. Assets should be bundled with your game executable in an organized and compressed format. Here's how you can approach this:

- **Asset Loading**: Implement a robust asset loading system that can locate and load assets from the game's package efficiently. This system should handle different asset types (textures, sounds, models) and file formats.

- **Asset Updates**: Plan for updates and patches by developing a mechanism for delivering new assets or updates to players. This can be crucial for fixing bugs or adding new content post-launch.

Version Control and Source Management

Use version control systems like Git to manage your game's source code and assets. This allows you to track changes, collaborate with team members, and maintain a history of your project's development. Additionally, consider using branching strategies to manage different versions or features of your game.

Distribution Channels

Decide where and how you want to distribute your game:

- **Online Stores**: Platforms like Steam, Epic Games Store, Apple App Store, Google Play, and others offer a convenient way to reach a broad audience. Be sure to follow their submission and review processes.

- **Your Website**: You can host your game on your website and sell it directly to players. This gives you more control but requires effective marketing and payment processing.

- **Physical Copies**: If you plan to release physical copies of your game, work with manufacturers and distributors to produce and distribute CDs, DVDs, or other physical media.

- **Demo and Free Versions**: Consider releasing a free demo or lite version of your game to attract players and encourage them to purchase the full version.

- **Community Platforms**: Engage with gaming communities, forums, and social media to build awareness and a player base for your game.

Distribution Packages

Prepare distribution packages that include everything needed to run the game on different platforms. These packages typically contain the game executable, assets, configuration files, and any necessary runtime libraries. Make sure that installation and launching instructions are clear for players.

Testing and Quality Assurance

Thoroughly test your game on various target platforms to ensure that it runs smoothly without issues. Perform testing on different hardware configurations to catch compatibility problems early. Consider creating a bug reporting system for players to report issues and collect feedback.

Documentation and Support

Provide clear documentation for players, including installation instructions, system requirements, gameplay guides, and troubleshooting tips. Offer customer support channels to assist players with technical issues or inquiries.

Marketing and Promotion

Plan your marketing and promotion strategies to reach your target audience effectively. This may involve creating a website, generating press releases, running social media campaigns, and reaching out to gaming influencers or reviewers for coverage.

Building and distributing your game requires careful planning and execution. By following these steps and considering platform-specific requirements, you can successfully share your game with the world and, hopefully, gain a satisfied player base.

Section 16.4: Marketing and Promotion Strategies

Marketing and promotion are crucial aspects of releasing a successful game. Even if you've created an outstanding game, it won't reach its full potential without an effective marketing strategy. In this section, we'll explore various strategies and considerations for marketing your game.

1. Create an Engaging Website

Build a dedicated website for your game. This serves as the central hub for information, updates, and downloads. Ensure that the website is visually appealing, mobile-friendly, and provides clear details about the game, including screenshots, videos, and a compelling description.

2. Utilize Social Media

Harness the power of social media platforms such as Twitter, Facebook, Instagram, and TikTok to connect with your audience. Regularly post updates, teasers, and engaging content related to your game. Interact with your followers and encourage them to share your posts.

3. Develop a Press Kit

Create a press kit that includes high-quality images, videos, press releases, and game information. This makes it easy for journalists, bloggers, and content creators to cover your game. Ensure that the press kit is easily accessible on your website.

4. Engage with Influencers and Reviewers

Identify gaming influencers and reviewers whose audience aligns with your game's target demographic. Reach out to them with review copies and promotional materials. Positive reviews and coverage from reputable sources can significantly boost your game's visibility.

5. Participate in Gaming Communities

Join gaming forums, subreddits, and other community platforms relevant to your game's genre. Actively engage in discussions, share your progress, and seek feedback from the community. Be respectful and avoid excessive self-promotion.

6. Run a Beta Test

Before the official launch, consider running a beta test or early access phase. This not only helps identify and fix issues but also generates buzz and interest among players. Encourage beta testers to provide feedback and report bugs.

7. Email Marketing

Collect email addresses from interested players and build a mailing list. Send out newsletters with updates, exclusive content, and promotional offers. Email marketing is a valuable tool for maintaining player engagement.

8. Collaborate with Other Developers

Collaborating with other indie developers can be mutually beneficial. You can cross-promote each other's games, share marketing strategies, and even collaborate on game bundles or events.

9. Launch on Multiple Platforms

Consider releasing your game on various platforms, including PC, Mac, Linux, consoles, and mobile devices. Each platform has its unique audience, and this broadens your reach.

10. Create a Launch Trailer

Craft an attention-grabbing launch trailer that showcases your game's best features. The trailer should be concise, visually appealing, and effectively communicate what makes your game special.

11. Run Contests and Giveaways

Organize contests and giveaways on social media platforms or your website. This encourages user engagement and can help expand your game's reach as participants share the contests with their friends.

12. Leverage Crowdfunding and Crowdsourcing

If applicable, consider using crowdfunding platforms like Kickstarter or Indiegogo to secure additional funding and build a community of backers. Crowdsourcing ideas and feedback can enhance your game's development.

13. Monitor Analytics and Adjust

Regularly monitor analytics to assess the effectiveness of your marketing efforts. Track website traffic, social media engagement, and conversion rates. Based on data, adjust your marketing strategy as needed.

14. Timing Matters

Plan your game's release carefully. Consider avoiding major releases from AAA titles or competitors. Research industry events and gaming conventions for opportunities to showcase your game.

15. Build Hype Before Launch

Generate excitement by building hype before your game's release. Teasers, countdowns, and sneak peeks can create anticipation and drive interest.

Remember that marketing is an ongoing effort, and it's essential to adapt to changing trends and audience preferences. Building a strong community around your game and maintaining player engagement are keys to long-term success.

Section 16.5: Supporting Your Game's Community

Supporting your game's community is a vital aspect of post-launch game development. A thriving community can lead to increased player engagement, word-of-mouth promotion, and long-term success. In this section, we'll explore strategies for effectively supporting your game's community.

1. Frequent Communication

Maintain open and frequent communication channels with your player community. Use social media, forums, and your game's website to share updates, news, and respond to player inquiries. Engaging with your community fosters a sense of involvement and trust.

2. Player Feedback

Encourage players to provide feedback, suggestions, and bug reports. Create a designated space, such as a forum or email address, where players can submit their thoughts. Actively listen to feedback and consider implementing player-suggested improvements.

3. Regular Updates

Continue to develop and improve your game post-launch. Release regular updates that address bugs, add new content, and enhance the player experience. Keep players excited by sharing your roadmap for upcoming features and improvements.

4. Community Events

Organize in-game events, challenges, or tournaments that encourage community participation. These events can boost player engagement, foster competition, and provide opportunities for players to connect with each other.

5. Player Support

Provide prompt and helpful customer support. Ensure that players have access to resources like FAQs, troubleshooting guides, and a support email. Address player issues and concerns professionally and promptly.

6. Community Moderation

If your game has online interactions, consider appointing community moderators or volunteers. They can help maintain a positive and respectful atmosphere in forums and chats, ensuring that discussions remain constructive.

7. Transparency

Be transparent about your development process, including challenges and setbacks. Sharing insights into your work can create a deeper connection with your community and help them understand the complexities of game development.

8. Reward Loyalty

Acknowledge and reward loyal players. Consider implementing loyalty programs, offering exclusive in-game items, or recognizing long-time community members. Showing appreciation can strengthen player commitment.

9. Engage on Social Media

Interact with your community on social media platforms regularly. Respond to comments, share player-created content, and create polls or surveys to involve players in decision-making processes.

10. Player-Created Content

Encourage and celebrate player-created content, such as fan art, mods, or user-generated levels. Showcase exceptional creations on your website or social media channels to inspire others.

11. Accessibility and Inclusivity

Ensure that your game is accessible to a diverse audience. Consider options for different languages, accessibility features, and input methods. Promote an inclusive and welcoming community environment.

12. Roadmap and Development Diaries

Maintain a public roadmap that outlines your future plans for the game. Share development diaries or behind-the-scenes content to keep players informed about ongoing work and upcoming features.

13. Regular Surveys

Conduct surveys or polls to gather community opinions on various aspects of your game. This can help guide your development decisions and demonstrate that you value player input.

14. Celebrate Milestones

Celebrate significant milestones, such as anniversaries or player achievements. Host special in-game events or offer limited-time rewards to mark these occasions.

15. Player-Developer Interaction

Consider hosting live Q&A sessions, developer streams, or in-game meetups. Direct interaction with players can create a stronger sense of community and connection.

Remember that building and maintaining a dedicated player community takes time and effort. By actively engaging with your community and valuing their input, you can create a loyal player base that continues to support your game long after its initial release.

Chapter 17: Handling Errors and Exception Handling

Section 17.1: Common Errors in Game Development

In game development, as in any software development field, encountering errors and issues is a common occurrence. Understanding these common errors and knowing how to address them is essential for creating stable and bug-free games. In this section, we'll explore some of the most prevalent errors and challenges you may encounter during game development and discuss strategies for effectively handling them.

1. Null Pointer Exceptions

Null pointer exceptions occur when you attempt to access a memory location that doesn't point to a valid object. These can lead to crashes or unexpected behavior in your game. To prevent null pointer exceptions, always initialize your pointers and use nullptr (in C++) or null (in some other languages) for empty pointers.

```cpp
// Initializing a pointer to nullptr
sf::RenderWindow* window = nullptr;
```

2. Memory Leaks

Memory leaks happen when your game allocates memory (e.g., with new or malloc) but fails to deallocate it with delete or free. Over time, this can lead to your game consuming more and more memory, potentially causing performance issues and crashes. Utilize smart pointers (e.g., std::shared_ptr in C++) or make sure to release allocated memory appropriately.

```cpp
// Using std::shared_ptr to manage memory automatically
std::shared_ptr<sf::Texture> texture = std::make_shared<sf::Texture>();
```

3. Resource Management

Improper resource management can lead to issues like missing textures or sounds. Ensure that you release resources when they're no longer needed, and use resource managers to load and unload assets efficiently.

```cpp
// Example of a simple texture manager
ResourceManager<Texture> textureManager;
sf::Texture* playerTexture = textureManager.load("player.png");
```

4. Crashes and Segmentation Faults

Crashes and segmentation faults can be caused by various issues, including invalid memory access, infinite loops, or stack overflows. Use debugging tools, such as breakpoints and stack traces, to identify the source of crashes and address them.

```cpp
// Using a breakpoint to pause execution for debugging
int value = 42;
if (value == 0) {
    // Set a breakpoint here to inspect variables and the call stack
}
```

5. Logic Errors

Logic errors occur when your game's code doesn't produce the intended behavior. These errors can be challenging to detect because they don't always result in crashes. To address logic errors, use thorough testing, including unit tests and playtesting, to identify and fix issues.

```
// Example of a logic error in collision detection
if (object1.intersects(object2)) {
    // Logic error: The collision condition is incorrect
    // Correct the collision logic to produce the desired behavior
}
```

6. **Performance Bottlenecks**

Performance issues like low frame rates or high CPU usage can negatively impact the
player experience. Use profiling tools to identify bottlenecks in your code and optimize
critical sections for better performance.

```
// Profiling performance with a profiler tool
Profiler profiler;
profiler.start();
// Code to be profiled
profiler.stop();
profiler.printResults();
```

7. **Multi-Threading Issues**

When using multi-threading in your game, synchronization issues such as data races and
deadlocks can occur. Employ proper thread synchronization mechanisms like mutexes or
locks to ensure thread safety.

```
// Using a mutex to protect a shared resource
std::mutex resourceMutex;
// Thread 1
resourceMutex.lock();
// Access and modify shared resource
resourceMutex.unlock();
// Thread 2
resourceMutex.lock();
// Access and modify shared resource
resourceMutex.unlock();
```

8. **Input Handling Bugs**

Input-related bugs can lead to unresponsive controls or unintended game behavior.
Implement robust input handling, including handling edge cases, to ensure a smooth player
experience.

```
// Example of handling input events
sf::Event event;
while (window.pollEvent(event)) {
    if (event.type == sf::Event::KeyPressed) {
        // Handle key press events
    }
}
```

9. Integration and Compatibility Issues

When integrating third-party libraries or deploying your game on various platforms, compatibility issues can arise. Thoroughly test your game on different configurations and platforms to ensure smooth deployment.

10. Inadequate Error Handling

Neglecting to handle errors gracefully can result in abrupt game terminations. Implement proper error handling, including exception handling in languages like C++, to provide informative error messages and avoid crashes.

```cpp
// Example of exception handling
try {
    // Code that may throw an exception
}
catch (const std::exception& e) {
    std::cerr << "An error occurred: " << e.what() << std::endl;
}
```

Understanding and addressing these common errors and challenges in game development is crucial for delivering a high-quality gaming experience. While errors are inevitable, a proactive and systematic approach to debugging and testing can

Section 17.2: Using Exception Handling in C++

Exception handling is a powerful mechanism in C++ that allows you to deal with runtime errors and exceptional situations gracefully. When an error occurs, C++ can throw an exception, and your code can catch and handle it. This section explores the fundamentals of exception handling in C++ and how it can be applied in game development.

Exception Basics

In C++, exceptions are objects that represent errors or exceptional conditions. When an error occurs, you can use the throw keyword to raise an exception. The exception is then propagated up the call stack until it's caught by an appropriate catch block.

Here's a simple example of throwing and catching an exception:

```cpp
#include <iostream>

void divide(int numerator, int denominator) {
    if (denominator == 0) {
        throw std::runtime_error("Division by zero is not allowed.");
    }
    int result = numerator / denominator;
    std::cout << "Result: " << result << std::endl;
}
```

```cpp
int main() {
    try {
        divide(10, 2);  // This will execute without exceptions
        divide(5, 0);   // This will throw an exception
    } catch (const std::exception& e) {
        std::cerr << "Exception: " << e.what() << std::endl;
    }
    return 0;
}
```

In the code above, the `divide` function checks if the denominator is zero and throws a `std::runtime_error` exception if it is. The `main` function catches exceptions using a try-catch block.

Catching Specific Exceptions

You can catch specific types of exceptions by specifying the exception type in the `catch` block. This allows you to handle different types of exceptions differently.

```cpp
#include <iostream>
#include <stdexcept>

void processFile(const std::string& filename) {
    // Attempt to open the file
    std::ifstream file(filename);

    if (!file.is_open()) {
        throw std::runtime_error("Failed to open file.");
    }

    // Process the file
    // ...
}

int main() {
    try {
        processFile("data.txt");
    } catch (const std::runtime_error& e) {
        std::cerr << "File error: " << e.what() << std::endl;
    } catch (const std::exception& e) {
        std::cerr << "An error occurred: " << e.what() << std::endl;
    }
    return 0;
}
```

In this example, the `processFile` function may throw a `std::runtime_error` if it fails to open the file. The `main` function catches this specific exception type and provides an appropriate error message.

Custom Exceptions

In game development, you may define custom exception classes to represent game-specific errors. These custom exceptions can inherit from `std::exception` or its derived classes and provide additional information about the error.

```cpp
#include <iostream>
#include <stdexcept>

class GameException : public std::runtime_error {
public:
    GameException(const std::string& message)
        : std::runtime_error(message) {}
};

void playGame() {
    // ...
    if (playerLost) {
        throw GameException("You lost the game.");
    }
    // ...
}

int main() {
    try {
        playGame();
    } catch (const GameException& e) {
        std::cerr << "Game error: " << e.what() << std::endl;
    } catch (const std::exception& e) {
        std::cerr << "An error occurred: " << e.what() << std::endl;
    }
    return 0;
}
```

In this example, the `GameException` class is a custom exception derived from `std::runtime_error`. It allows you to distinguish game-related exceptions from other exceptions.

RAII (Resource Acquisition Is Initialization)

RAII is a programming idiom in C++ that promotes resource management through object lifetimes. It's particularly useful in game development for managing resources like memory, files, and graphics objects.

For example, you can create a custom RAII class to manage file resources. When an instance of this class is created, it opens the file, and when the instance goes out of scope, it automatically closes the file.

```cpp
#include <iostream>
#include <fstream>
```

```cpp
#include <stdexcept>

class FileResource {
public:
    FileResource(const std::string& filename)
        : file(filename) {
        if (!file.is_open()) {
            throw std::runtime_error("Failed to open file.");
        }
    }

    ~FileResource() {
        if (file.is_open()) {
            file.close();
        }
    }

    // Other methods for reading and writing to the file
private:
    std::ifstream file;
};

void processFile(const std::string& filename) {
    FileResource fileResource(filename);
    // Automatically manages file resources
    // ...
}

int main() {
    try {
        processFile("data.txt");
    } catch (const std::exception& e) {
        std::cerr << "An error occurred: " << e.what() << std::endl;
    }
    return 0;
}
```

In

Section 17.3: SFML's Exception Handling Mechanism

SFML, the Simple and Fast Multimedia Library, provides its own exception handling mechanism for reporting and handling errors and exceptions that can occur during its usage. Understanding how SFML handles exceptions is important for robust error management in your game development projects.

Exception Types in SFML

SFML uses its own exception hierarchy for reporting errors and exceptional situations. Some of the commonly used exception types in SFML include:

- sf::Exception: The base class for all SFML exceptions. It derives from std::runtime_error and provides a consistent interface for all SFML-related exceptions.

- sf::FileNotFound: Thrown when an expected file is not found.

- sf::InvalidParameter: Raised when an invalid parameter is passed to an SFML function.

- sf::UnsupportedFeature: Indicates that a feature is not supported by the current system or configuration.

- sf::GlResourceError: An exception related to OpenGL resources. For example, this may be raised when texture loading fails.

Throwing and Catching SFML Exceptions

When using SFML, you may encounter these exceptions when, for instance, loading resources or working with windows and graphics. It's essential to handle these exceptions gracefully to provide informative error messages to the user and ensure that your game doesn't crash unexpectedly.

Here's an example of throwing and catching an SFML exception when loading a texture:

```cpp
#include <SFML/Graphics.hpp>
#include <iostream>

int main() {
    sf::RenderWindow window(sf::VideoMode(800, 600), "SFML Exception Handling");

    try {
        sf::Texture texture;
        if (!texture.loadFromFile("non_existent_texture.png")) {
            throw sf::FileNotFound("Texture not found!");
        }
        // Use the texture here
    } catch (const sf::Exception& e) {
        std::cerr << "SFML Exception: " << e.what() << std::endl;
    }

    while (window.isOpen()) {
        sf::Event event;
        while (window.pollEvent(event)) {
            if (event.type == sf::Event::Closed) {
```

```
                window.close();
            }
        }

        window.clear();
        // Draw your game here
        window.display();
    }

    return 0;
}
```

In this example, an `sf::Texture` is loaded from a non-existent file, causing an `sf::FileNotFound` exception. The code catches this exception, prints an error message, and continues execution, preventing the program from crashing.

Handling SFML Exceptions Proactively

To handle SFML exceptions effectively, it's crucial to be proactive in error checking and validation. For example, before attempting to draw a sprite or play a sound, you should ensure that the associated resources are loaded successfully. This proactive approach can help avoid unexpected exceptions during gameplay.

Here's a simplified example of checking whether a texture was loaded successfully before using it:

```
sf::Texture texture;
if (texture.loadFromFile("image.png")) {
    // Use the texture for rendering
} else {
    std::cerr << "Failed to load texture!" << std::endl;
}
```

By validating the success of resource loading operations, you can handle potential exceptions before they occur, providing a smoother player experience.

Custom Exception Handling

In addition to SFML's built-in exception types, you can create your custom exceptions that derive from `sf::Exception` or its subclasses to represent game-specific errors. Custom exceptions can provide additional context and information about the error and help you differentiate between different types of exceptions in your game.

```
#include <SFML/Graphics.hpp>
#include <iostream>

class GameException : public sf::Exception {
public:
    explicit GameException(const std::string& message)
        : sf::Exception(message) {}
```

```cpp
};

int main() {
    try {
        if (/* some game-specific error condition */) {
            throw GameException("A custom game error occurred!");
        }
    } catch (const GameException& e) {
        std::cerr << "Custom Game Exception: " << e.what() << std::endl;
    } catch (const sf::Exception& e) {
        std::cerr << "SFML Exception: " << e.what() << std::endl;
    }

    return 0;
}
```

In this example, the GameException class is derived from sf::Exception. This custom exception class allows you to raise and catch game-specific exceptions while still handling SFML exceptions when necessary.

Logging and Debugging

When handling exceptions in your game, consider using a logging system to record error messages and debug information. This can be invaluable for diagnosing and fixing issues during development and providing meaningful error reports to players in production builds. Logging frameworks like Log4cpp or custom logging classes can help you manage logs effectively.

In summary, SFML's exception handling mechanism provides a robust way to report and handle errors and exceptional situations in your game development projects. By understanding SFML's exception hierarchy, proactively checking for potential exceptions, creating custom exceptions when needed, and implementing logging and debugging mechanisms, you can enhance the robustness and reliability of your games while providing a better user experience.

Section 17.4: Debugging Tools for Error Resolution

Debugging is an essential part of game development, and having the right tools at your disposal can greatly simplify the process of identifying and resolving errors in your code. In this section, we'll explore some debugging tools and techniques that can be valuable when working with SFML-based projects.

1. Integrated Development Environments (IDEs)

Modern IDEs like Visual Studio, CLion, and Code::Blocks offer powerful debugging capabilities for C++ development. These IDEs allow you to set breakpoints, inspect variables, and step through your code line by line. When working with SFML, you can utilize these features to trace the execution of your game and pinpoint issues.

2. SFML's Debug Mode

SFML provides a debug mode that can help you catch common mistakes and issues early in development. When SFML is compiled in debug mode, it performs additional checks and provides more descriptive error messages when something goes wrong. Be sure to use debug builds of SFML during development to take advantage of this feature.

3. Error Logging

Logging is a valuable technique for tracking the flow of your program and capturing important information during runtime. You can use popular C++ logging libraries like Log4cpp or create your custom logging system. By logging relevant information, such as function calls, variable values, and error messages, you can gain insights into the behavior of your game and identify problematic areas.

4. Assertions

Assertions are conditional statements that you can use to check assumptions in your code. In C++, you can employ the assert macro to assert conditions and halt the program's execution if the condition is false. This is particularly useful for catching logic errors and validating input data during development.

```
#include <cassert>

int divide(int a, int b) {
    assert(b != 0 && "Division by zero is not allowed");
    return a / b;
}
```

5. Static Code Analysis Tools

Static code analysis tools like Clang-Tidy and PVS-Studio can automatically analyze your codebase for potential issues, code style violations, and other problems. These tools can help you identify issues that might not be apparent during manual code review.

6. Memory Debugging

Memory-related issues, such as memory leaks and invalid memory access, can be particularly challenging to debug. Tools like Valgrind (on Linux) and AddressSanitizer (available with modern compilers) can help you detect and fix memory-related problems efficiently.

7. Profiling

Profiling tools allow you to analyze the performance of your game and identify bottlenecks. Profilers like gprof, Perf, and Intel VTune Profiler can help you optimize your code for better frame rates and responsiveness.

8. Unit Testing

Unit testing involves creating automated test cases to verify the correctness of individual components or functions in your code. Unit testing frameworks like Google Test can help you catch regressions and ensure that changes to your code don't introduce new bugs.

9. Version Control Systems

Using version control systems like Git enables you to track changes to your codebase, collaborate with other developers, and revert to previous versions if issues arise. Git also provides branching and merging capabilities, making it easier to experiment with new features without affecting the stable version of your game.

10. Community and Forums

Don't underestimate the power of the developer community. Online forums, discussion boards, and communities related to SFML and C++ game development can be valuable resources for getting help, sharing knowledge, and learning from others' experiences.

In conclusion, debugging tools and techniques are essential for maintaining the stability and reliability of your SFML-based game projects. Whether you're using integrated development environments, error logging, assertions, static code analysis, memory debugging, profiling, unit testing, version control, or community support, having a well-rounded debugging strategy can save you time and frustration during development. Debugging is not just about finding and fixing bugs; it's also about improving the overall quality and performance of your games.

Section 17.5: Strategies for Error Prevention

While debugging is crucial for identifying and fixing errors in your game code, preventing errors in the first place is an even better approach. In this section, we'll explore strategies and best practices for error prevention in your SFML game development projects.

1. Code Reviews

Regular code reviews by your team members or peers can help identify potential issues early in the development process. Code reviews promote collaboration, knowledge sharing, and the spotting of coding errors and oversights.

2. Coding Standards

Adhering to a consistent coding style and following established coding standards can make your code more readable and less error-prone. Consider adopting widely-accepted coding standards like the Google C++ Style Guide or the C++ Core Guidelines.

3. Static Analysis Tools

Integrate static code analysis tools into your development workflow. These tools can automatically scan your codebase for common programming mistakes, code smells, and potential issues. Popular tools include Clang-Tidy and PVS-Studio.

4. Testing and Test-Driven Development (TDD)

Write automated tests for critical parts of your code using a testing framework like Google Test. Test-Driven Development (TDD) encourages writing tests before writing code, which can help ensure that your code functions correctly and reliably.

5. Code Linters

Utilize code linters, which are tools that analyze your code for potential errors, style violations, and best practice adherence. Tools like ESLint (for JavaScript) and ClangFormat (for C++) can help maintain code quality.

6. Documentation

Thoroughly document your code, including comments, function descriptions, and usage examples. Clear documentation can make it easier for you and others to understand and use your code correctly.

7. Code Reviews

Regular code reviews by your team members or peers can help identify potential issues early in the development process. Code reviews promote collaboration, knowledge sharing, and the spotting of coding errors and oversights.

8. Version Control

Use version control systems like Git to track changes to your codebase. This allows you to roll back to previous versions if errors are introduced and provides a safety net for your codebase.

9. Error Handling and Validation

Implement robust error handling and input validation throughout your code. Check for errors and invalid data inputs at every entry point and provide meaningful error messages or exceptions to guide users and developers in understanding and resolving issues.

10. Refactoring

Regularly refactor your code to keep it clean and maintainable. Refactoring involves restructuring code without changing its external behavior. This can help eliminate hidden bugs and improve code quality.

11. Use Modern C++ Features

Leverage modern C++ features and libraries that provide safer alternatives to older practices. Features like smart pointers, the Standard Library, and the C++ Standard Template Library (STL) can help reduce common programming errors.

12. Continuous Integration (CI)

Set up a CI pipeline that automatically builds and tests your code whenever changes are pushed to your version control repository. CI systems can catch errors early and ensure that your codebase remains in a working state.

13. Dependency Management

Manage external dependencies carefully. Keep your dependencies up to date and ensure that they are compatible with your project. Outdated or incompatible dependencies can introduce errors into your code.

14. Education and Training

Invest in ongoing education and training for your development team. Staying up-to-date with the latest programming techniques, best practices, and tools can help prevent common errors.

By incorporating these strategies into your SFML game development workflow, you can reduce the likelihood of introducing errors and improve the overall quality and reliability of your game projects. While no development process can completely eliminate errors, a proactive approach to error prevention can save you time and effort in the long run.

Chapter 18: Exploring Advanced SFML Features

Section 18.1: Particle Systems and Special Effects

In game development, creating captivating visual effects is essential for engaging gameplay and immersing players in your world. SFML provides tools for implementing particle systems and other special effects, allowing you to add dynamic and visually appealing elements to your games.

What Are Particle Systems?

Particle systems are a technique used to simulate and render a large number of small, individual entities known as particles. These particles can represent various visual elements, such as fire, smoke, rain, sparks, or magical spells. By combining multiple particles and controlling their behavior over time, you can create complex and realistic effects.

Implementing Particle Systems in SFML

SFML offers features and classes that make it relatively straightforward to implement particle systems. Here's a high-level overview of the steps involved:

1. **Particle Representation:** Choose a graphical representation for your particles. This can be simple shapes, sprites, or custom textures. SFML's `sf::CircleShape` or `sf::RectangleShape` can be useful for basic shapes.

2. **Particle Data:** Define data structures to store information about each particle, such as position, velocity, color, and lifetime.

3. **Initialization:** Initialize a set of particles with appropriate initial values. This typically includes setting their positions, velocities, colors, and lifetimes.

4. **Update Logic:** In each frame of your game loop, update the state of each particle. This includes moving particles according to their velocities, changing colors or sizes over time, and decreasing their lifetimes.

5. **Rendering:** Render the particles to the screen. For each particle, use the particle's position and graphical representation to draw it on the screen.

6. **Particle Pool:** To efficiently manage particles, you can use a particle pool that reuses particles as they expire, reducing the need for memory allocation and deallocation.

Particle System Parameters

To create visually appealing effects, you can adjust various parameters of your particle system, including:

- **Emission Rate:** Control how frequently new particles are created.
- **Particle Lifetime:** Determine how long each particle remains visible before fading out.
- **Particle Velocity:** Set the initial speed and direction of particles.
- **Particle Size:** Define the size of particles over their lifetime.
- **Color Variation:** Add variety to particles by changing their colors or transparency.
- **Gravity and Forces:** Simulate forces like gravity, wind, or turbulence to affect particle motion.
- **Collision Detection:** Implement collision detection between particles and other game elements.

Example: Creating a Simple Fire Effect

Here's a basic example of how you can create a simple fire effect using SFML's particle system:

```cpp
#include <SFML/Graphics.hpp>

int main() {
    sf::RenderWindow window(sf::VideoMode(800, 600), "Simple Fire Effect");

    // Create a particle system
    sf::ParticleSystem particles(1000);
    particles.setEmitter(sf::Vector2f(400, 550));
    particles.setTexture(sf::Texture::create(2, 2));

    // Set particle properties
    particles.setParticleLifetime(sf::seconds(2));
    particles.setParticleColor(sf::Color::Red);
    particles.setParticleSize(sf::Vector2f(10, 10));
    particles.setEmissionRate(100);

    sf::Clock clock;

    while (window.isOpen()) {
        sf::Event event;
        while (window.pollEvent(event)) {
            if (event.type == sf::Event::Closed) {
                window.close();
            }
        }

        // Update particle system
        sf::Time elapsed = clock.restart();
        particles.update(elapsed);

        window.clear();
        window.draw(particles);
```

```
        window.display();
    }

    return 0;
}
```

In this example, particles are emitted from a specific point at the bottom of the window, creating a simple fire-like effect. You can customize and enhance this effect by adjusting various parameters and adding additional logic.

By exploring particle systems and special effects in SFML, you can elevate the visual quality of your games and create captivating experiences for your players. Experiment with different settings and combine particle systems with other SFML features to achieve stunning results.

Section 18.2: Working with Shaders

Shaders are powerful tools in modern game development that allow you to manipulate the graphics pipeline to create stunning visual effects. SFML provides support for shaders, making it possible to apply real-time, dynamic effects to your game graphics. In this section, we'll explore how to work with shaders in SFML.

What Are Shaders?

Shaders are small programs written in a shader language, such as GLSL (OpenGL Shading Language). They run on the GPU and are responsible for processing each pixel or vertex during rendering. Shaders can be categorized into two main types:

1. **Vertex Shaders:** These shaders operate on each vertex of a 3D model and are used to transform their positions and attributes.

2. **Fragment Shaders:** Also known as pixel shaders, these shaders work on each pixel of the screen and are used to calculate the final color of the pixel.

The Shader Class in SFML

SFML provides the sf::Shader class, which allows you to load and apply shaders to your game graphics. To use shaders, you'll typically follow these steps:

1. **Create or Load Shader Files:** Write or obtain shader code written in GLSL. SFML supports both vertex and fragment shaders.

2. **Load the Shaders:** Use sf::Shader::loadFromFile() to load shader files into your program.

3. **Set Shader Parameters:** You can set uniform variables in your shader to control the appearance of your graphics.

4. **Apply the Shader:** Use `sf::RenderWindow::draw()` with a `sf::Shader` object to apply the shader to your graphics.

Here's an example of how to create a simple shader that inverts the colors of your game screen:

```
#include <SFML/Graphics.hpp>

int main() {
    sf::RenderWindow window(sf::VideoMode(800, 600), "SFML Shader Example");

    // Load the shader from a file
    sf::Shader shader;
    shader.loadFromFile("invert_colors.frag", sf::Shader::Fragment);

    while (window.isOpen()) {
        sf::Event event;
        while (window.pollEvent(event)) {
            if (event.type == sf::Event::Closed) {
                window.close();
            }
        }

        // Apply the shader
        window.clear();
        window.draw(sf::Sprite(sf::Texture())); // Draw a sprite to apply the shader
        window.display();
    }

    return 0;
}
```

In this example, we load a fragment shader from a file named "invert_colors.frag" and apply it to a blank sprite. The shader inverts the colors of everything drawn on the screen.

Creating Custom Shaders

To create custom shaders, you'll need to learn GLSL and experiment with different effects. You can use shaders for a wide range of effects, including grayscale, sepia, blur, distortion, and more. There are many online resources and tutorials available to help you get started with GLSL shader programming.

Shaders are a powerful tool for adding visual depth and uniqueness to your games. By mastering shader programming, you can take your game's graphics to the next level and create visually stunning experiences for players.

Section 18.3: Audio Effects and 3D Sound

Audio is a crucial aspect of game development, as it can greatly enhance the overall player experience. In this section, we will explore audio effects and 3D sound in SFML. These features allow you to create immersive soundscapes and provide players with a more realistic audio experience.

Audio Effects

SFML provides support for various audio effects that can be applied to sounds and music. These effects allow you to modify the audio in real-time, creating unique and dynamic sound experiences for your games. Some common audio effects supported by SFML include:

- **Reverb:** Simulates sound reflections in enclosed spaces, creating a sense of space and depth.

- **Equalization (EQ):** Adjusts the balance of different frequency components in audio, allowing you to emphasize or de-emphasize specific frequencies.

- **Pitch Shifting:** Alters the pitch (frequency) of audio, creating effects like slow motion or high-pitched voices.

- **Distortion:** Adds harmonic overtones to audio, creating a "distorted" sound often used in music and games.

- **Chorus:** Simulates the sound of multiple voices or instruments playing the same thing, creating a richer and more spacious audio texture.

To apply audio effects in SFML, you'll typically follow these steps:

1. **Create or Load Audio Files:** Prepare your sound or music files that you want to apply effects to.

2. **Create Sound Buffers:** Load your audio files into `sf::SoundBuffer` objects.

3. **Apply Effects:** Create an `sf::Sound` or `sf::Music` object and apply effects using the appropriate functions, such as `sf::Sound::setReverb()`, `sf::Sound::setPitch()`, or `sf::Sound::setDistortion()`.

4. **Play the Audio:** Finally, play the sound or music to hear the applied effects.

Here's an example of applying reverb to a sound:

```
#include <SFML/Audio.hpp>

int main() {
    sf::RenderWindow window(sf::VideoMode(800, 600), "SFML Audio Effects Exam
```

```
ple");

    // Load an audio file into a sound buffer
    sf::SoundBuffer buffer;
    buffer.loadFromFile("sample.wav");

    // Create a sound and set its buffer
    sf::Sound sound;
    sound.setBuffer(buffer);

    // Create a reverb effect
    sf::SoundBufferRecorder recorder;
    sf::SoundBuffer reverbBuffer;
    recorder.start();
    sound.play();
    recorder.stop();
    reverbBuffer = recorder.getBuffer();
    sound.setBuffer(reverbBuffer);

    while (window.isOpen()) {
        sf::Event event;
        while (window.pollEvent(event)) {
            if (event.type == sf::Event::Closed) {
                window.close();
            }
        }

        window.clear();
        // Draw your game here
        window.display();
    }

    return 0;
}
```

In this example, we load an audio file, play it, and apply a reverb effect to it.

3D Sound

SFML also supports 3D sound, allowing you to position sounds in a 3D space and simulate realistic audio spatialization. To use 3D sound in SFML, you'll need to consider factors such as the position, direction, and attenuation of sounds relative to the listener's position. By adjusting these parameters, you can create realistic soundscapes where sounds appear to come from different directions and distances.

Here's a brief overview of key concepts in 3D sound:

- **Listener:** The listener is a virtual point in the 3D space that represents the player's position and orientation. Sounds are positioned relative to the listener.

- **Sound Source:** A sound source is an object that emits sound. You can position sound sources in 3D space and control their properties.

- **Attenuation:** Attenuation is the decrease in volume as a sound source moves away from the listener. It simulates the real-world phenomenon where distant sounds are quieter.

To work with 3D sound in SFML, you'll use the `sf::Listener` class to set the listener's position and orientation and the `sf::Sound` class to set the position and properties of sound sources.

Here's an example of using 3D sound in SFML:

```cpp
#include <SFML/Audio.hpp>

int main() {
    sf::RenderWindow window(sf::VideoMode(800, 600), "SFML 3D Sound Example");

    // Create a sound buffer and load an audio file
    sf::SoundBuffer buffer;
    buffer.loadFromFile("sample.wav");

    // Create a sound source and set its buffer
    sf::Sound sound;
    sound.setBuffer(buffer);

    // Set listener's position
    sf::Listener::setPosition(0.0f, 0.0f, 0.0f);

    while (window.isOpen()) {
        sf::Event event;
        while (window.pollEvent(event
```


Section 18.4: Implementing Custom Rendering Techniques

In game development, custom rendering techniques are often employed to achieve specific visual effects or optimizations that can't be achieved through standard rendering pipelines alone. This section explores the concept of implementing custom rendering techniques using SFML.

Understanding Custom Rendering

Custom rendering techniques involve manipulating the rendering process to achieve desired results. These techniques can encompass various aspects of graphics programming, such as shader programming, post-processing effects, and advanced rendering algorithms.

Here are some common scenarios where custom rendering techniques can be useful:

1. **Shader Effects:** Shaders are programs that run on the GPU and can be used to create a wide range of visual effects, including dynamic lighting, shadows, water simulation, and more. SFML provides support for shader programming through the `sf::Shader` class, allowing you to apply custom shaders to your game objects.

2. **Post-Processing:** Post-processing effects are applied to the final rendered frame to enhance or modify the image. Examples include blur, bloom, color correction, and depth-of-field effects. You can implement post-processing by rendering the scene to a texture, applying a shader, and then rendering the textured quad to the screen.

3. **Advanced Rendering Algorithms:** Some games require specialized rendering algorithms to achieve specific visual styles or optimizations. Examples include cel shading for a cartoon-like appearance, voxel-based rendering for blocky worlds, and ray tracing for highly realistic graphics. Implementing such techniques often involves customizing the rendering pipeline.

Using Shaders in SFML

SFML provides a straightforward way to use shaders for custom rendering effects. To utilize shaders, follow these steps:

1. **Create Shader Programs:** You'll need to write shader programs in GLSL (OpenGL Shading Language). SFML supports both vertex and fragment shaders. Use `sf::Shader::loadFromFile()` to load shader files.

2. **Pass Data to Shaders:** Shaders can receive data in the form of uniform variables. Use `sf::Shader::setUniform()` to pass data like textures, colors, or matrices to your shaders.

3. **Apply Shaders:** To apply a shader, use `sf::RenderStates` when drawing shapes or sprites. Set the `shader` member of `sf::RenderStates` to your shader object.

Here's a simplified example of using shaders to create a grayscale effect:

```cpp
#include <SFML/Graphics.hpp>

int main() {
    sf::RenderWindow window(sf::VideoMode(800, 600), "SFML Shader Example");

    // Create a shader
    sf::Shader grayscaleShader;
    grayscaleShader.loadFromFile("grayscale.frag", sf::Shader::Fragment);
```

```
    // Create a sprite with a texture
    sf::Texture texture;
    texture.loadFromFile("image.png");
    sf::Sprite sprite(texture);

    while (window.isOpen()) {
        sf::Event event;
        while (window.pollEvent(event)) {
            if (event.type == sf::Event::Closed) {
                window.close();
            }
        }

        // Apply the grayscale shader to the sprite
        sprite.setShader(&grayscaleShader);

        window.clear();
        window.draw(sprite);
        window.display();
    }

    return 0;
}
```

In this example, we load a fragment shader (grayscale.frag) that converts the colors of the sprite to grayscale. We then apply this shader to the sprite before drawing it.

Custom Rendering and Optimization Techniques

Custom rendering goes beyond shaders and can involve optimizing rendering pipelines, implementing novel algorithms, and creating unique visual effects. Depending on your project's requirements, you may need to dive deep into graphics programming to achieve the desired results.

When implementing custom rendering techniques, consider factors like performance, compatibility, and maintainability. Properly documented and well-structured code is essential for managing complex rendering systems. Additionally, profiling tools can help identify bottlenecks and areas for optimization in your custom rendering code.

Conclusion

Custom rendering techniques play a crucial role in game development, allowing you to create visually stunning effects and optimize performance. SFML's support for shaders and flexible rendering pipelines empowers developers to implement a wide range of custom rendering solutions to meet their specific needs. Whether you're creating dynamic lighting, post-processing effects, or entirely unique rendering styles, SFML provides the tools to bring your vision to life.

Section 18.5: Advanced Input and Event Handling

Advanced input and event handling are essential aspects of game development, allowing you to create responsive and interactive gameplay experiences. In this section, we will delve into more advanced techniques for managing user input and handling events efficiently in your SFML games.

Custom Input Handling

While SFML provides straightforward input handling through its event system, complex games may require custom input processing. Here are some scenarios where custom input handling becomes necessary:

1. **Combination Keys:** Detecting complex key combinations or sequences, such as "Ctrl + Shift + A," to trigger specific in-game actions.

2. **Input Buffering:** Implementing input buffering systems that queue and process player inputs in a specific order, ensuring precise control over game mechanics.

3. **Input Mapping:** Allowing players to customize keybindings by mapping specific actions to their preferred keys or gamepad buttons.

4. **Input Filtering:** Filtering out unwanted input, like ignoring multiple rapid clicks of a button or preventing input from specific devices.

To implement custom input handling, you can maintain your data structures to store and process input events or use third-party input management libraries that offer advanced input handling capabilities.

Handling Gamepad and Joystick Input

Supporting gamepad and joystick input is crucial for ensuring your game can be played on various platforms and offers a more immersive gaming experience. SFML provides straightforward support for handling gamepad and joystick input.

To work with gamepad and joystick input in SFML, follow these steps:

1. **Enumerate Connected Devices:** Use `sf::Joystick::isConnected()` to check if a joystick is connected to the system. You can use this information to dynamically adapt your game's input handling.

2. **Reading Input:** Poll the joystick for input states using `sf::Joystick::getAxisPosition()` and `sf::Joystick::isButtonPressed()`. These functions allow you to read analog and digital inputs from the device.

3. **Mapping Input:** Map joystick buttons and axes to in-game actions or controls. Create a mapping system that associates joystick inputs with specific actions or functions in your game.

Here's a simplified example of handling gamepad input:

```cpp
#include <SFML/Graphics.hpp>

int main() {
    sf::RenderWindow window(sf::VideoMode(800, 600), "SFML Gamepad Example");

    while (window.isOpen()) {
        sf::Event event;
        while (window.pollEvent(event)) {
            if (event.type == sf::Event::Closed) {
                window.close();
            }
        }

        // Check if a joystick is connected
        if (sf::Joystick::isConnected(0)) {
            // Check button 0 (usually the A button on Xbox-style controllers)
            if (sf::Joystick::isButtonPressed(0, 0)) {
                // Perform an action in your game
            }

            // Read the position of the left stick
            float xAxis = sf::Joystick::getAxisPosition(0, sf::Joystick::X);
            float yAxis = sf::Joystick::getAxisPosition(0, sf::Joystick::Y);

            // Use the axis values for character movement, camera control, etc.
        }

        window.clear();
        // Draw your game elements here
        window.display();
    }

    return 0;
}
```

In this example, we check if a joystick (identified by index 0) is connected and read button and axis inputs. You can use these inputs to control various aspects of your game.

Input Handling Libraries

For more complex input handling needs, you might consider using third-party input handling libraries that offer additional features, such as input rebinding, input buffering, and customizable input actions. Popular libraries like "SFML-Input" or "ImGui" can simplify input management in your projects.

Conclusion

Advanced input and event handling are crucial for creating engaging and responsive gameplay experiences in your SFML games. Whether you need to implement custom input handling for complex actions or support gamepad and joystick input for diverse platforms, SFML provides the tools to achieve these goals. Additionally, third-party input handling libraries can further streamline input management and customization in your games. Mastering input handling is essential for fine-tuning the player's interaction with your game and ensuring a satisfying gaming experience.

Chapter 19: Game Development Best Practices

Section 19.1: Code Structure and Organization

Proper code structure and organization are fundamental aspects of writing maintainable, scalable, and efficient game code. As your game project grows, a well-structured codebase becomes increasingly important to avoid chaos and development bottlenecks. In this section, we'll explore best practices for structuring your game's code.

1. Modularization

Breaking your code into smaller, modular components is essential. Each module should have a well-defined purpose and encapsulate related functionality. For example, you can have separate modules for graphics rendering, physics simulation, and user interface management.

```
// Example directory structure:
// ├── src
// │   ├── Graphics
// │   │   ├── Renderer.cpp
// │   │   └── TextureManager.cpp
// │   ├── Physics
// │   │   ├── CollisionSystem.cpp
// │   ├── UI
// │   │   ├── UIManager.cpp
// ├── main.cpp
```

2. Object-Oriented Design

Utilize object-oriented principles to structure your game. Create classes for game objects, characters, and other entities. Inheritance and composition can help you model complex relationships between objects.

```cpp
class GameObject {
public:
    virtual void Update(float deltaTime) = 0;
    virtual void Render(sf::RenderWindow& window) = 0;
};

class Player : public GameObject {
public:
    void Update(float deltaTime) override {
        // Player-specific logic here
    }
    void Render(sf::RenderWindow& window) override {
        // Rendering code
```

```
    }
};
```

3. Separation of Concerns

Follow the principle of "separation of concerns." Keep different aspects of your game, such as rendering, input handling, and game logic, separated. This makes your codebase more modular and easier to maintain.

```cpp
// Separate game logic from rendering
class Game {
public:
    void Update(float deltaTime) {
        // Game logic here
    }
};

class Renderer {
public:
    void Render(const Game& game, sf::RenderWindow& window) {
        // Rendering code
    }
};
```

4. Dependency Management

Manage dependencies carefully. Use dependency injection or dependency inversion principles to decouple modules and make your code more flexible. Avoid global variables and prefer passing dependencies explicitly.

```cpp
class GameManager {
public:
    GameManager(Renderer& renderer, PhysicsEngine& physics)
        : renderer(renderer), physics(physics) {}

    void Update(float deltaTime) {
        // Use renderer and physics here
    }

private:
    Renderer& renderer;
    PhysicsEngine& physics;
};
```

5. Documentation and Comments

Document your code thoroughly. Include comments that explain complex algorithms, functions, and classes. A well-documented codebase is easier for you and your team to understand and maintain.

6. Consistent Naming Conventions

Adhere to consistent naming conventions for variables, functions, and classes. This improves code readability. For example, use camelCase for variables and PascalCase for class names.

7. Version Control

Use version control systems like Git to track changes to your codebase. Version control allows you to collaborate with others, track progress, and revert changes if necessary.

8. Coding Standards

Adopt coding standards or style guides for your project. Consistency in code style across your team makes the codebase more readable and maintainable.

9. Refactoring

Regularly review and refactor your codebase to remove redundancy, improve performance, and enhance maintainability. Code reviews with team members can help identify areas for improvement.

Conclusion

A well-structured and organized codebase is the foundation of successful game development. It enhances collaboration among team members, simplifies debugging and maintenance, and allows your game to grow without becoming unmanageable. By following these best practices, you can create a codebase that stands the test of time and ensures a smooth development process.

Section 19.2: Code Version Control with Git

Code version control is a critical aspect of game development, ensuring that your project's history is tracked, enabling collaboration with team members, and providing a safety net for changes. Git, a widely-used distributed version control system, plays a central role in managing your game project's source code.

What Is Git?

Git is a distributed version control system designed to handle everything from small to large projects with speed and efficiency. It keeps track of changes to your codebase, allowing multiple developers to work on the same project simultaneously. Git also provides a history of changes, simplifying collaboration, and error recovery.

Setting Up Git

To get started with Git, you need to install it on your development machine. You can download the Git installer from the official website (https://git-scm.com/downloads) and follow the installation instructions for your platform.

After installing Git, you should configure your identity by setting your username and email address using the following commands:

```
git config --global user.name "Your Name"
git config --global user.email "your.email@example.com"
```

Initializing a Git Repository

To start using Git in your game project, you'll need to initialize a Git repository in your project's root directory. Open a terminal, navigate to your project folder, and run the following command:

```
git init
```

This command initializes an empty Git repository in your project directory.

Staging and Committing Changes

Once your Git repository is set up, you can start tracking changes to your code. Git uses a staging area to prepare changes for commit. To stage changes, use the `git add` command followed by the file or files you want to include in the next commit:

```
git add filename.cpp
```

After staging your changes, you can commit them with a descriptive message:

```
git commit -m "Add new feature"
```

This creates a commit with your staged changes and a meaningful commit message.

Branching and Merging

Git allows you to work on different branches of your codebase simultaneously. You can create a new branch using the `git branch` command and switch to it with `git checkout`:

```
git branch new-feature
git checkout new-feature
```

You can make changes on the new branch, commit them, and then merge the branch back into the main development branch (usually called `main` or `master`) using the `git merge` command.

Remote Repositories

Git enables collaboration with others by allowing you to work with remote repositories hosted on platforms like GitHub, GitLab, or Bitbucket. You can clone a remote repository to your local machine using `git clone` and push your changes to the remote repository using `git push`.

Git is a powerful tool for managing your game development project. By using Git, you can keep track of changes, collaborate with team members, and maintain a history of your codebase's evolution. Learning Git and adopting version control best practices can greatly enhance your game development workflow.

Section 19.3: Documentation and Comments

Documentation and comments are essential elements of game development that contribute to the clarity, maintainability, and collaboration of your project. In this section, we'll explore the importance of documentation and comments in game development and provide guidelines for their effective use.

Why Documentation and Comments Matter

1. **Understanding Code:** Code can become complex, and even the developer who wrote it may struggle to understand it after some time. Documentation and comments serve as a guide to help developers understand the purpose and functionality of various code sections.

2. **Collaboration:** Game development often involves working with a team of programmers, artists, designers, and other professionals. Well-documented code and comments facilitate collaboration by ensuring that team members can comprehend and work with the codebase.

3. **Maintainability:** Over time, you'll likely need to update and maintain your game. Proper documentation and comments make it easier to identify and fix issues, add new features, and improve performance without introducing errors.

4. **Onboarding New Developers:** When new team members join your project, clear documentation and comments allow them to get up to speed quickly. This reduces the learning curve and improves productivity.

Guidelines for Documentation

Here are some guidelines for creating effective documentation in your game project:

1. **Function and Class Documentation:** Document functions and classes with descriptions of their purpose, input parameters, and return values. Use clear and concise language.

2. **File-Level Documentation:** Include an overview at the top of each source code file describing the file's contents, author, creation date, and any relevant information.

3. **Code Style Guide:** Establish a code style guide for your project that specifies naming conventions, code formatting, and commenting standards. Consistency in coding style improves readability.

4. **Inline Comments:** Use inline comments to explain complex logic, unusual code choices, or any part of the code that might be less intuitive to others. Avoid over-commenting; comments should add value.

5. **Change Logs:** Maintain a change log or commit messages that summarize the purpose of each change, especially in version control systems like Git. This provides historical context for code changes.

Example of Good Documentation

Here's an example of a well-documented function:

```
/**
 * @brief Calculates the sum of two numbers.
 *
 * This function takes two integers and returns their sum.
 *
 * @param a The first integer.
 * @param b The second integer.
 * @return The sum of `a` and `b`.
 */
int CalculateSum(int a, int b) {
    // Add the two numbers
    return a + b;
}
```

In this example, the function is documented with a description of its purpose, input parameters, and return value. The comments clarify the operation performed within the function.

Conclusion

Documentation and comments are crucial components of maintaining a well-structured and collaborative game development project. By following best practices and integrating documentation into your coding workflow, you can enhance the quality of your code and make it more accessible to your team members and future maintainers.

Section 19.4: Collaborative Development Strategies

Collaborative development is a fundamental aspect of game development, especially for larger projects involving multiple team members. In this section, we'll explore collaborative development strategies and best practices to ensure a smooth workflow and successful project outcomes.

Version control systems are essential tools for collaborative game development. They allow multiple developers to work on the same project simultaneously while tracking changes, resolving conflicts, and maintaining a history of project versions. Here are key concepts related to VCS:

1. **Git**: Git is one of the most popular VCS used in the game development industry. It allows developers to create branches for specific features or bug fixes, merge changes, and collaborate effectively.

2. **GitHub and GitLab**: These platforms provide hosting for Git repositories and offer features like issue tracking, pull requests, and collaboration tools. They are commonly used for open-source and private game projects.

3. **Branching Strategy**: Define a branching strategy that suits your project. Common strategies include feature branches, release branches, and hotfix branches. Consistency in branching simplifies collaboration.

4. **Commit Messages**: Write clear and descriptive commit messages that explain the purpose of each change. Include references to issues or tasks if applicable.

Code reviews are integral to maintaining code quality and consistency in a collaborative game development environment. Here's how to conduct effective code reviews:

1. **Peer Reviews**: Have team members review each other's code before merging it into the main branch. This helps catch errors and ensures adherence to coding standards.

2. **Feedback**: Provide constructive feedback during code reviews. Focus on code clarity, efficiency, and adherence to project standards.

3. **Code Linters**: Use code linters or static analysis tools to automatically identify code issues and enforce coding standards.

Managing tasks and issues is crucial for organizing and tracking progress in a collaborative project:

1. **Task Management Tools**: Utilize task management tools like Trello, Asana, or JIRA to create and assign tasks, set priorities, and track progress.

2. **Issue Tracking**: Use issue tracking systems to log and prioritize bugs, feature requests, and other project-related issues.

Effective communication is essential for successful collaboration:

1. **Regular Meetings**: Schedule regular team meetings to discuss progress, challenges, and goals. Video conferences or chat applications can facilitate remote communication.

2. **Documentation**: Maintain project documentation, including design documents, coding guidelines, and style guides. This ensures that team members are on the same page.

3. **Instant Messaging**: Use instant messaging tools like Slack or Discord for real-time communication and quick problem-solving.

Continuous Integration and Deployment (CI/CD)

Implement CI/CD pipelines to automate building, testing, and deploying the game. This ensures that changes are thoroughly tested and deployed consistently.

Conclusion

Collaborative game development can be highly rewarding, but it requires effective tools, processes, and communication. By utilizing version control systems, conducting code reviews, managing tasks and issues, and fostering open communication, your team can work together seamlessly to create a successful game project.

Section 19.5: Keeping Your Game Up-to-Date

Keeping your game up-to-date is a crucial aspect of game development, ensuring that your players receive the best experience and that your project remains relevant. In this section, we'll explore strategies and practices for updating your game efficiently and effectively.

1. Regular Updates

Regular updates are essential to keep players engaged and interested in your game. Plan and schedule updates that bring new content, features, or improvements. This can include adding new levels, characters, items, or fixing known issues.

2. Player Feedback

Listen to player feedback through community forums, reviews, and social media. Act on constructive feedback to improve the game and show your commitment to the player community. Consider implementing a feedback system within the game itself.

3. Bug Fixes and Patches

Addressing bugs and issues promptly is critical. Maintain a list of known bugs and prioritize them based on severity and impact. Release patches and updates to fix these issues, and communicate the changes in patch notes.

4. Balancing and Tweaking

Game balancing is an ongoing process. Analyze gameplay data and player feedback to adjust difficulty levels, character abilities, or item statistics. Keep an eye on gameplay analytics to make informed decisions.

5. Compatibility Updates

As technology evolves, your game may need compatibility updates to work seamlessly on new platforms or operating system versions. Stay informed about platform updates and ensure your game remains compatible.

6. Security Updates

Security is a concern in online and multiplayer games. Regularly update your game to address security vulnerabilities. Consider implementing security measures such as encryption and authentication.

7. Content Expansion

Consider expanding your game with downloadable content (DLC) or expansions. This can provide additional revenue streams and keep players engaged with new content.

8. Community Engagement

Engage with your player community through social media, forums, and live streams. Announce upcoming updates, seek player input, and create a sense of community around your game.

9. Version Control

Use version control systems like Git to manage different versions of your game. This ensures that you can access and modify previous versions if needed.

10. Testing and Quality Assurance

Before releasing updates, thoroughly test them to avoid introducing new bugs or issues. Automated testing, beta testing, and player testing are valuable approaches.

11. Marketing and Promotion

Promote your updates effectively. Build anticipation with teaser trailers, blog posts, and social media announcements. Leverage your existing player base to spread the word.

12. Long-Term Roadmap

Create a long-term roadmap for your game's development. Outline your vision for future updates and expansions, so players know what to expect.

Conclusion

Keeping your game up-to-date is a continuous process that requires dedication and responsiveness. By staying in touch with your player community, addressing issues promptly, and delivering new and exciting content, you can maintain a thriving game that players will continue to enjoy for years to come.

Chapter 20: Beyond SFML: Next Steps in Game Development

Section 20.1: Exploring Other Game Development Libraries

In this final chapter, we will explore the world of game development beyond SFML. While SFML is an excellent library for 2D game development, there are many other libraries, frameworks, and engines that cater to different types of games and platforms. Let's take a look at some of the options you can consider as you advance in your game development journey.

1. Unity

Unity is one of the most popular and versatile game engines available. It supports both 2D and 3D game development and offers a user-friendly interface, a powerful scripting system, and a vast asset store. Unity is cross-platform and supports multiple programming languages, including C#. It's an excellent choice for creating a wide range of games, from mobile apps to console and PC titles.

2. Unreal Engine

Unreal Engine is another top-tier game engine known for its stunning 3D graphics and robust features. It's widely used in the game industry and is known for its visual scripting system, Blueprints, which makes game development accessible to non-programmers. Unreal Engine is suitable for creating high-end games and has powerful graphics capabilities.

3. Godot Engine

Godot Engine is an open-source game engine that's gaining popularity. It's known for its simplicity and ease of use. Godot uses its scripting language, GDScript, which is similar to Python, making it beginner-friendly. It supports 2D and 3D game development and has a thriving community.

4. Phaser

Phaser is a JavaScript framework for creating 2D games that run in web browsers. It's lightweight and ideal for making HTML5 games. Phaser is popular among indie developers and is excellent for web-based games that can be played on various devices.

5. LibGDX

LibGDX is a Java-based game development framework that supports 2D and 3D games. It's cross-platform, making it suitable for Android, iOS, desktop, and web game development. LibGDX is known for its performance and flexibility.

6. Love2D

Love2D is a framework for creating 2D games using the Lua programming language. It's lightweight, easy to learn, and great for rapid game prototyping. Love2D is open-source and has an active community.

7. Cocos2d-x

Cocos2d-x is a C++ framework for building 2D games that run on multiple platforms, including iOS, Android, Windows, and more. It's known for its efficiency and is often used for mobile game development.

8. GameMaker Studio

GameMaker Studio is a game development platform that allows you to create 2D and 3D games using its drag-and-drop interface or its scripting language, GML. It's beginner-friendly and suitable for creating both simple and complex games.

9. Lumberyard

Amazon Lumberyard is a free game engine that specializes in creating immersive 3D games with cloud integration. It's ideal for building multiplayer and online games.

10. Custom Engines

For advanced developers, creating a custom game engine tailored to your specific project's needs is an option. This requires a deep understanding of programming, mathematics, and graphics rendering.

Remember that the choice of a game development tool largely depends on your project's requirements, your team's expertise, and your target platforms. As you explore these alternatives, you'll find the one that best suits your game development goals. Additionally, learning different engines and frameworks can expand your skill set and open up new opportunities in the game development industry.

Section 20.2: Learning Advanced Game Development Topics

Now that you've gained experience with SFML and explored other game development tools in the previous section, it's time to delve into more advanced game development topics. These topics will help you take your game development skills to the next level and tackle more complex projects.

1. Game Physics and Simulations

Understanding game physics is crucial for creating realistic and engaging games. You'll learn about concepts like collision detection, rigid body dynamics, and particle systems. Libraries like Box2D and NVIDIA PhysX can help you implement physics in your games.

```cpp
// Example of using Box2D for physics simulation
b2World world(b2Vec2(0.0f, -9.81f)); // Create a Box2D world with gravity

// Create dynamic bodies, fixtures, and shapes
b2BodyDef bodyDef;
bodyDef.type = b2_dynamicBody;
b2Body* dynamicBody = world.CreateBody(&bodyDef);

b2PolygonShape dynamicBox;
dynamicBox.SetAsBox(1.0f, 1.0f);

b2FixtureDef fixtureDef;
fixtureDef.shape = &dynamicBox;
fixtureDef.density = 1.0f;
fixtureDef.friction = 0.3f;

dynamicBody->CreateFixture(&fixtureDef);

// Simulate the world over time
float32 timeStep = 1.0f / 60.0f;
int32 velocityIterations = 6;
int32 positionIterations = 2;

for (int32 i = 0; i < 60; ++i) {
    world.Step(timeStep, velocityIterations, positionIterations);
}
```

2. Advanced Graphics and Shaders

To create visually stunning games, you'll explore advanced graphics techniques. This includes using shaders for effects like lighting, shadows, and post-processing. Learning OpenGL or Vulkan can provide you with low-level access to the GPU.

```glsl
// Example of a simple vertex shader
#version 330 core

layout(location = 0) in vec3 inPosition;

uniform mat4 projection;
uniform mat4 view;
uniform mat4 model;

void main() {
```

```
    gl_Position = projection * view * model * vec4(inPosition, 1.0);
}
```

3. Artificial Intelligence (AI)

Implementing AI in games is essential, especially for non-player characters (NPCs). You'll study pathfinding algorithms (A*), decision trees, behavior trees, and neural networks. Libraries like OpenAI's Gym and TensorFlow can be beneficial.

```python
# Example of a simple A* pathfinding algorithm in Python
def astar(graph, start, end):
    open_set = PriorityQueue()
    open_set.put((0, start))
    came_from = {}
    g_score = {node: float('inf') for node in graph}
    g_score[start] = 0

    while not open_set.empty():
        _, current = open_set.get()

        if current == end:
            path = []
            while current in came_from:
                path.append(current)
                current = came_from[current]
            return path[::-1]

        for neighbor in graph[current]:
            tentative_g_score = g_score[current] + dist_between(current, neighbor)

            if tentative_g_score < g_score[neighbor]:
                came_from[neighbor] = current
                g_score[neighbor] = tentative_g_score
                f_score = tentative_g_score + heuristic(neighbor, end)
                open_set.put((f_score, neighbor))

    return None
```

4. Multiplayer and Networked Games

Building multiplayer games involves dealing with networking, synchronization, and server-client architecture. You'll learn about protocols like TCP and UDP and libraries like RakNet and Photon.

```csharp
// Example of basic client-server communication in C# using sockets
// Server side
TcpListener server = new TcpListener(IPAddress.Any, 12345);
server.Start();
```

```
TcpClient client = server.AcceptTcpClient();
NetworkStream stream = client.GetStream();
byte[] data = new byte[256];

int bytesRead = stream.Read(data, 0, data.Length);
string message = Encoding.ASCII.GetString(data, 0, bytesRead);
Console.WriteLine($"Received: {message}");

// Client side
TcpClient client = new TcpClient("server_ip", 12345);
NetworkStream stream = client.GetStream();
string message = "Hello, server!";
byte[] data = Encoding.ASCII.GetBytes(message);

stream.Write(data, 0, data.Length);
```

5. Game Design and Storytelling

Mastering game design principles is vital for creating enjoyable and engaging games. You'll delve into topics like player experience (UX), level design, narrative design, and user interface (UI) design.

These advanced topics will equip you with the skills and knowledge needed to tackle complex game development projects and contribute to the ever-evolving world of game development. Remember that practice, experimentation, and continuous learning are key to becoming a proficient game developer.

Section 20.3: Joining Game Development Communities

Becoming a part of game development communities can be immensely beneficial for your growth as a game developer. These communities provide opportunities to learn, collaborate, and stay updated on industry trends. Here are some reasons why joining game development communities is valuable:

1. Networking and Collaboration

Game development communities are hubs of talented individuals, including programmers, artists, designers, and writers. By participating in these communities, you can network with like-minded people, potentially finding collaborators for your projects. Collaborative game development can lead to richer and more diverse games.

2. Learning and Sharing Knowledge

Game development communities are treasure troves of knowledge. Developers often share their experiences, insights, and tutorials. You can learn from the challenges and successes of others. Don't hesitate to ask questions and seek advice when you encounter difficulties in your projects.

3. Feedback and Playtesting

Communities offer a platform to showcase your games and gather feedback. Playtesting is essential for refining your games and improving the user experience. Constructive criticism from fellow developers and players can help you identify areas for improvement.

4. Staying Informed

The game development industry evolves rapidly, with new technologies and trends emerging regularly. Being part of a community ensures you stay informed about the latest developments. You can discuss emerging tools, engines, and techniques with experienced developers.

5. Game Jams and Challenges

Many game development communities organize game jams and challenges. These events provide opportunities to test your skills, experiment with new ideas, and create games within tight timeframes. Participating in such events can be a fun and educational experience.

6. Portfolio and Exposure

Sharing your work in game development communities can help you build a portfolio and gain exposure. If your projects are well-received, they may attract the attention of publishers, investors, or potential employers.

7. Emotional Support

Game development can be a challenging and sometimes solitary endeavor. Communities offer emotional support and camaraderie. Sharing your struggles and achievements with others who understand your passion can boost your motivation and resilience.

Here are some popular game development communities and platforms you can consider joining:

- **Unity Community:** If you're using Unity, their official forums and the Unity Connect platform are great places to start.
- **Unreal Engine Forums:** Unreal Engine developers can engage with the community on the Unreal Engine forums.
- **Indie Game Developers on Reddit:** Reddit has several subreddits dedicated to game development, including r/gamedev and r/indiegamedev.
- **GitHub:** Collaborate on open-source game projects and share your own on GitHub.
- **Game Jams:** Participate in online and local game jams, such as Ludum Dare and Global Game Jam.
- **Discord Communities:** Many game development-focused Discord servers host discussions, events, and collaboration opportunities.

Remember that active participation and respectful interaction are key to making the most of these communities. By joining these networks, you can enhance your skills, make valuable connections, and contribute to the vibrant world of game development.

Section 20.4: Pursuing Game Development as a Career

Pursuing a career in game development is an exciting and challenging journey. It offers opportunities to work on innovative projects, unleash your creativity, and contribute to a rapidly growing industry. Whether you dream of becoming an indie developer, joining a game studio, or specializing in a specific role, here's how you can start and progress in a game development career:

1. Education and Skill Development

Formal Education

Many game developers begin their careers by pursuing a degree in computer science, game design, or a related field. These programs provide a solid foundation in programming, mathematics, and game development principles.

Self-Learning

You can also teach yourself game development through online courses, tutorials, and resources. Platforms like Coursera, Udemy, and Unity Learn offer valuable courses in game development.

2. Choose Your Specialization

Game development encompasses various roles, including:

- **Game Programmer:** Responsible for coding game mechanics, systems, and functionality.
- **Game Designer:** Focuses on game mechanics, level design, and player experience.
- **Game Artist:** Creates visual assets like characters, environments, and animations.
- **Game Writer:** Develops narratives, dialogues, and storylines.
- **Game Producer:** Manages project timelines, resources, and team coordination.

Identify your strengths and interests to determine the right specialization for you.

3. Build a Portfolio

Create a portfolio showcasing your skills and projects. Include personal game projects, contributions to open-source games, or mods you've created. A portfolio demonstrates your capabilities to potential employers or collaborators.

4. Gain Practical Experience

Participate in game jams, internships, or freelance projects to gain practical experience. Working on real projects helps you apply your knowledge, learn industry practices, and build a network.

5. Networking

Attend industry events, conferences, and game development meetups. Networking can lead to job opportunities and collaborations. Online platforms like LinkedIn and Twitter are also valuable for connecting with professionals.

6. Job Search

When seeking employment in the game industry, research game studios, job openings, and requirements. Tailor your resume and cover letter to highlight relevant skills and experiences. Consider applying to entry-level positions to kickstart your career.

7. Indie Game Development

If you aspire to be an indie developer, start small and gradually work on larger projects. Platforms like Steam, itch.io, and mobile app stores provide avenues to publish your games independently.

8. Continuous Learning

Game development is an ever-evolving field. Stay updated with the latest technologies and trends, and continuously improve your skills.

9. Be Resilient

The game development industry can be competitive and demanding. Be prepared for setbacks and rejections. Persistence and a growth mindset are essential.

10. Seek Mentorship

Finding a mentor in the game industry can provide guidance and insights. Reach out to experienced developers and ask for mentorship or advice.

11. Diversify Your Portfolio

Consider exploring different genres and platforms. Diversity in your portfolio can make you a more versatile developer.

12. Game Development Communities

As discussed in the previous section, joining game development communities can provide support, knowledge sharing, and opportunities to showcase your work.

Pursuing game development as a career is a journey that requires dedication, passion, and continuous learning. Whether you aim to create indie games, work for renowned studios, or specialize in a specific aspect of game development, staying committed to your goals can lead to a fulfilling and rewarding career in this dynamic industry.

Section 20.5: Conclusion and Final Thoughts

Congratulations on completing this comprehensive guide to game development with SFML! As we conclude this journey, let's recap the key takeaways and offer some final thoughts.

Recap of Key Takeaways

Throughout this book, you've learned a wide range of topics related to game development with SFML:

- **SFML Fundamentals:** You started with the basics, understanding what SFML is and why it's a great choice for game development. You also learned how to set up your development environment on various platforms.

- **C++ Basics:** We covered essential C++ concepts that are crucial for SFML development, ensuring you have a solid foundation in programming.

- **SFML Essentials:** You created your first SFML project, learned how to work with windows, display graphics, and handle user input. You built your own games, from Pong to Tic-Tac-Toe.

- **Advanced Graphics:** You delved into more advanced graphics techniques, including text and fonts, sprites and textures, animation, special effects, and user interface design.

- **Game Development Strategies:** We explored game development strategies, debugging and testing techniques, and how to extend and enhance your games with features like sound, music, and multiplayer support.

- **Input Handling:** You learned how to handle various input devices, from keyboards and mice to gamepads and touchscreen controls.

- **Data Management:** We covered the crucial topic of saving and loading game data, including managing game saves, file I/O, and data storage in JSON/XML format.

- **Networking:** You got an introduction to networking in game development, including building multiplayer games, online leaderboards, chat systems, and server-client communication.

- **Optimization:** We discussed performance optimization techniques, memory management, GPU acceleration, input lag reduction, and tips for achieving smooth gameplay.

- **Publishing Your Game:** You learned how to prepare your game for distribution, package game assets, build and distribute your game, and employ marketing and promotion strategies.

- **Handling Errors:** We explored common errors in game development, exception handling in C++, SFML's exception handling mechanism, debugging tools, and strategies for error prevention.

- **Advanced SFML Features:** You looked into advanced SFML features, including particle systems, shaders, audio effects, 3D sound, custom rendering techniques, and advanced input and event handling.

- **Best Practices:** We discussed game development best practices, including code structure, version control with Git, documentation, collaborative development strategies, and keeping your game up-to-date.

- **Next Steps:** Finally, we explored what lies beyond SFML, including other game development libraries, advanced game development topics, joining game development communities, pursuing game development as a career, and offered some concluding thoughts.

Final Thoughts

As you conclude your journey through this book, remember that game development is a dynamic and ever-evolving field. The skills and knowledge you've gained will serve as a strong foundation for your game development endeavors, whether you're creating indie games, contributing to a game studio, or exploring other aspects of the industry.

Stay curious and continue learning, experiment with new ideas, collaborate with fellow developers, and most importantly, have fun creating games! Game development is not just a profession; it's a passionate pursuit of art, entertainment, and storytelling.

Thank you for choosing this guide as your companion in your game development journey. We wish you the best of luck in all your game development endeavors, and we can't wait to see the incredible games you create. Happy coding!

www.ingramcontent.com/pod-product-compliance
Lightning Source LLC
LaVergne TN
LVHW051322050326
832903LV00031B/3314